The Triune God
in Christian Thought
and Experience

James A. Fowler

C.I.Y. Publishing
P.O. Box 1822
Fallbrook, CA 92088

THE TRIUNE GOD
IN CHRISTIAN THOUGHT AND EXPERIENCE

© Copyright 2013 by James A. Fowler

Published by C.I.Y. Publishing
P.O. Box 1822
Fallbrook, California 92088-1822

Printed in the United States of America

ISBN – 978-1-929541-46-1

TABLE OF CONTENTS

FOREWORD

The content of this study was first delivered at the Dan Stone Memorial Retreat held at the Fatima Renewal Center of the St. Pius X Seminary just north of Dalton, PA from May 24-26, 2013. If I recall correctly, this was the seventeenth consecutive year that I have spoken at this gathering, and I have come to know and love the participants who gather year after year from across the United States and Canada.

When formatting the teaching into written book-form, I have attempted to retain some of the personal characteristics of the spoken presentation, rather than restructuring the comments into more formal and academic theological text-form. The addenda illustrations at the conclusion of this book were originally used as the visual projections for the participants at the Retreat.

It is my prayer that these words might be used of God to speak to the hearts of those who read them, drawing them ever deeper into intimate fellowship with Father, Son and Holy Spirit.

James A. Fowler
September, 2013

INTRODUCTION

Early in the history of the Christian faith there was an intense awareness that the Christian understanding of God was unique and different from any other view of God in the religions of the world. Jesus claimed to be the Son of God who was integrally related to God the Father and empowered by the Spirit of God. In addition, the early Christians understood that the relationships of the Triune God were the means by which individuals in the human race could interact with God, partake of the very life of the Triune God, and express the loving character of the Triune God.

Early ecumenical councils of the church attempted to explain the uniqueness of the relations of the Triune God, formulating their explanations in creedal statements such as the Nicene Creed, which was expanded at the Council of Constantinople in A.D. 381. Discussions of the workings and purposes of the Father, Son, and Holy Spirit remained a "hot iron" issue in the early centuries of the church, but over the process of time the Christian doctrine of the Trinity was allowed to stagnate and become a sterile academic assertion. It was always regarded as a cardinal doctrine of Christian orthodoxy, but it came to be viewed as a purely formal doctrinal tenet, a speculative teaching about the Christian God. The concept of the Trinity became detached from ordinary Christian life, a teaching no longer integrally tied to God's relational life with us and our life with one another.

The Protestant Reformation of the sixteenth century did very little to ignite or amplify the distinct Christian emphasis on the Triune God. In fact, Luther's successor, Melanchthon, wrote, "There is no reason why we should spend much labor over the topics of God, His Unity, and Trinity," thus dismissing a renewed consideration of the integral and vital relational dynamics of the Triune God and the Christian community.

The Enlightenment "age of reason" in the 17th and 18th centuries only served to throw a blanket of skepticism over the Christian doctrine of the Trinity, elevating the human reasoning of science and mathematics as the utmost criteria for determination of human understanding, and relegating Trinitarian discussion to the realm of illegitimacy and superstition.

With such a legacy of Christian thought behind us, and the sad state of affairs in the Trinitarian awareness of the modern Church, this thesis calls for a renewed discussion and rethinking of the distinctively Christian God. We are in dire need of a radical change in how contemporary Christians perceive of the Triune God, Father, Son, and Holy Spirit, and the implications of the Trinity for the revitalization of the Christian community.

This study will be developed in three parts. These three parts are identified by three Greek words: *theologia, oikonomia,* and *koinonia* (cf. *Addendum A*), three rhyming words that will provide a comprehensive perspective of the interactive relationship between the tri-personal divine Being and human beings. These three words have been a part of Christian conversation since the earliest years of the Christian faith – almost 2000 years. Most are aware that the New Testament, the new covenant literature of the Christian faith, was written in the Greek language, the *koine* (common) Greek language of the people of the Eastern Mediterranean region. The earliest participants in the Christian Church spoke Greek, and these three words were major terms that they used in their explanations of God and His interactions with human beings. The Eastern Orthodox segment of Christianity still retains the use of the Greek language in their theology and liturgy to this very day, and these Greek words are particularly common in their conversations, though still used by Roman Catholic and Protestant scholars also.

The Greek word *theologia* is the word from which we get the word "theology." It is formed from two Greek words: *Theos* = God, and *Logos* = word, the latter being the word from which we get "logic," which has to do with "words about," the study of, and considerations of, in this case, God. We will be using it to refer to human considerations and understanding of God, who is, of course, above and beyond our finite thinking – and thus not fully comprehensible.

The Greek word *oikonomia* is the word from which we get the word "economy." That tends to throw us off track, because "economy" usually refers to financial and monetary concerns in modern usage. The Greek word *oikonomia* comes from 2 Greek words: *oikos* = household, and *nomos* = law. It had to do with the rule, administration or management of the activities of the household. In Christian conversations it pertains to the activities and workings of God in human history. Paul used *oikonomia* in I Tim. 1:4 to refer to "the administration of God," and in Eph. 1:10 to refer to "an administration suitable to the fullness of the times, that is, the summing up of all things in Christ." We will be using it as Paul used it, to refer to the administrative workings of God in human history; i.e. God's Self-revelation in His Son, Jesus Christ, and His redemptive actions.

The Gk. word *koinonia* is derived from the Greek word *koine*, which means "common." We previously mentioned that *koine* Greek was the common language of the people in the Eastern Mediterranean. *Koinonia* has to do with fellowship, partnership, communion, or participation in a relationship that is built around what the personal beings have in common. I John 1:3, for example, uses the word *koinonia* in the phrase, "our fellowship is with the Father, and with His Son, Jesus Christ," and four verses later in I John 1:7 the text mentions our "fellowship with one another." That is how we will be using the word *koinonia*, to refer to our personal relationship of participation with the Triune God, and with one another in the Christian community, which by the way, means "common unity" in the "fellowship of faith," in the Church.

When we have examined these three categories to see what they tell us of the Triune God, then we will need to consider the correlation and interaction of these categories, and note the struggles and differing interpretations that have led to discussions and dissensions throughout Christian history.

Theologia

We commence with the Greek word, *theologia*, to consider the "human considerations of God" who is beyond human understanding. For this reason alone the human considerations of God have often been abstract, speculative, and conjectural, the finite attempting to understand the infinite, physical man attempting to understand the God who is Spirit (cf. John 4:24).

Human beings have universally sought to explain a metaphysical being above and beyond themselves. This can only be attributable to the human recognition that men are not gods unto themselves (humanism), and that there must necessarily be a divine being superior to, and having more comprehensive power, than do human beings. Granted, this is merely a logical argument of necessity based on aspiration, but the vast spectrum of human hope gives credence to the assertion of a universal human desire to relate to the God who is superior to them. This is same type of argument C. S. Lewis utilized in his book, *Mere Christianity*, "If I find in myself a desire which no experience in this world can satisfy, the most probable explanation is that I was made for another world."

In this study of *theologia*, we are going to bypass the long history of human belief in polytheism – the existence of many gods. We will also pass over the concepts of pantheism and panentheism, that everything is god, or god is in everything. We will focus on monotheistic considerations of God. The English word "monotheism" is derived from two Greek words: *monos* = one, and *theos* = god. "Monotheism" was first utilized as a word in English literature by Thomas More (1614-1667). Early in human history, however, there is record of several people groups that developed various monotheistic concepts of a supreme force or being.

Predating the religions of Confucianism and Taoism, traditional Chinese religion centered on the worship of *Shangdi* (上帝), signifying "ultimate power," often conceptualized as the celestial emperor, and usually translated into English as "god." This divine entity was viewed as an impersonal omnipotent force, at the same time allowing for lesser gods and spirits who could carry out the will of *Shangdi*. This Chinese conception was not fully monotheistic, but carried with it the idea of a singular spiritual power, thought to be invested in their earthly emperors.

The Hindu religion, on the other hand, has had a form of monistic monotheism since the second millennium B.C. The "supreme spirit" in Vedic thought is identified as *Brahman*, regarded as omnipotent and all-pervading. In pantheistic form *Brahman* is identical to the universe, but in pan*entheistic* form *Brahman* is thought to contain all things, but not to be considered as identical with everything. The "true self" of every individual, called the *atman*, is generally considered to be indistinct from the *Brahman* – thus the designation "monistic monotheism," wherein all "being" is compressed in one god, or all that IS is God!

The Hebrew peoples are the earliest known civilization of human beings that espoused a concept of a singularly personal monotheistic God. Identifying Himself as *YHWH* (Hebrew יהוה – cf. Exod. 3:14, often Anglicized as Jehovah), the Jewish God revealed himself as the singular "God of Israel" who would not tolerate the worship of any other gods (Exod. 20:2-4). The

Shema statement from Deuteronomy 6:4 states, ""Hear, O Israel! The Lord is our God, the LORD is one!" Judaism was primarily a nationalistic ethnic religion that was not accepting of the *goyim* (foreign nations) that were not of the Jewish race. Though *Yahweh* was regarded as a monadic monotheistic deity, Judaism was functionally a form of ethnic ethical monotheism wherein *Yahweh* dictated a singularly acceptable code of behavior, which for the Jewish religion was centered in the Mosaic Law and its regulations of performance in exchange for expected divine blessings and protection.

Islam was developed in the seventh century (A.D. 610) when Muhammad (*circa* 570-632 A.D.) formulated an amalgam of religious thought combining Judaism, Christianity, and concepts from regional tribal religions. The Muslim god, *Allah*, is regarded to be the all-powerful and all-knowing creator, sustainer, and judge of the universe – singular (*tawhid*) and unique (*wahid*). The central assertion of Muslims is, "There is no god but *Allah*, and Muhammad is his messenger." The Islamic god is a power-based deity, requiring adherence to the deterministic "will of *Allah*" in all things. This is an adapted form of monadic monotheism with a militant assertion of exclusivity. Let us be very clear that the Muslims realize that their god is not the same as the Christian God. The Koran explicitly states, "Say not 'trinity,' say, "he Allah is one ... and none is like him," and goes on to explicitly deny that Allah has a son. Monotheistic religions in general do not necessarily serve the same god, as is the popular perception of many!

Western thought, in general, finds much of its origins in the early Greek philosophers. Though Plato (c. 424-348 B.C.) lived in a polytheistic culture with a pantheon of gods, and some of his teachings reflect such presuppositions, he philosophically proposed the concepts of "absolute truth" and "absolute good" in the formulation of "The One" (Tò "Ev), the ultimate, comprehensive Form or Being from which all appearances are but shadows. Plato's singular, timeless, unchanging ideological Idea could only be known through abstract contemplation. It was not personal, thus non-relational, and merely a conceptual construct that served as a singular, foundational underpinning for the ideal forms of truth, right, justice, beauty, etc. Plato's idea of "The One" was not technically monotheistic for he does not refer to it as "god," but his philosophical concept of a mono-ideal Form was easily accommodated to their particular monotheistic explanations of God by later Jewish and Christian thinkers.

The philosophical method employed by Plato in his speculative contemplation of the singular and perfect Ideal is referred to as the *a priori* process, meaning that prior to the experiential observation of any criteria one mentally projects and deduces the logical form and ideal that must necessarily exist to give expression to everything else. What results from this *a priori* methodology has been referred to as a system of "substantialist metaphysics," meaning that substantial and essential ontological realities are projected and postulated as underlying all physical phenomena. These comprise the ground of all Being (*ousia*), i.e., what the original archetype is projected to be in its very Being or ontological Form. (*cf. Addendum B*).

Whenever humans employ Plato's speculative projection in reference to the ultimate reality, the mental conception of a mono-metaphysical *noumenon* is but the logical deduction of the human mind. Perhaps we could say that the commencement of Genesis is reversed: "In the beginning, man created god in the deductions of his mind." The philosophical ideal of the essential substance(s) that are hypothesized as the categorical or conceptual core of all reality are but speculations of a superlative conceptualization comprising the best that the human mind can reason.

In addition to the many superlatives attributed to this mono-ideal Form that Plato proposed, subsequent thinkers using the *a priori* method throughout history added a whole list of attributes by negation. The One utmost Being or Form was identified and described by what it was not: immutable (unchanging), impassible (not moody, or subject to suffering), indivisible (simple, can't be partitioned), immovable (not fickle, steadfast), ineffable (beyond description), independent (non-contingent in its intrinsic aseity), immense, eternal, infinite (beyond space and time), immaterial (Spirit), etc. Conversely, others later added the omni-attributes of omnipotence (all-powerful), omniscience (all-knowing), and omnipresence (everywhere present), to note but a few.

The result, when the Platonic philosophical Ideal was adapted by accommodation to Jewish or Christian concepts of a personal monotheistic God, was that the ultimate, supreme Being was conceptualized in a big mental box of idealized superlatives: god in a box, and a little box, at that, no bigger than the best that humans could conceive in their human craniums.

Plato's most famous student, Aristotle (384–322 B.C.), retained the philosophical ideal of an ultimate ontological reality with its substantialist metaphysical postulates, but chose an antithetical methodology for approaching the awareness of the essential substances of reality. (*cf. Addendum C*). Instead of Plato's *a priori* method, Aristotle employed an *a posteriori* method. Whereas Plato projected hypothetical concepts of the absolute Ideal prior to any subjective observation of evidence, Aristotle chose to observe the after-effects (*post* = after) of the manifestations and appearances of physical phenomena in order to surmise how the metaphysical archetype might be explained. Commencing with the evidentiary or experiential phenomena, Aristotle sought to reason backwards, after the fact, to the possible origins of what he was observing or experiencing. This is more in line with what we would call "the scientific method" of thought in modern times, being an *a posteriori* consideration of the observable evidence.

The differing reasoning processes utilized by Plato and Aristotle are often identified as the contrast between *deductive* reasoning and *inductive* reasoning. While Plato would *deductively* project a conceptual ideal arguing from the universal to the particular, from the general to the specific, from the intangible to the tangible, and from the abstract to the concrete, Aristotle chose to begin with the physical phenomena that he could subjectively perceive and then *inductively* reason back to the origin and cause, from the particular to the universal, from the specific to the general, from the tangible to the intangible, and from the concrete to the abstract.

The antithetical, yet complementary, rational methods of the two foremost Greek philosophers, Plato and Aristotle, can be contrastively illustrated by visualizing Plato's "BIG BOX" of the Ideal projected Forms that comprise the Being of "The One." Aristotle, on the other hand, went outside of the box to observe the physical manifestations in order to inductively determine what concepts should consequently be placed in the "box" of metaphysical substantialist categories of the "ultimate being." Whereas Plato mentally constructed patterned ideas and forms that served as an archetype or prototype for all reality, Aristotle wanted to perceptually observe the material manifestations of matter that were the ectype that came "out of" the archetype, and then surmise the essence of real "being." Plato commenced with the metaphysical spiritual and soulical concepts that he projected to be objectively apprehended by the *noumena* of human thought. Aristotle thought it more reasonable to begin with the physical phenomena of the natural processes of the things in the world, and then draw subjective conclusions concerning the necessity and source of their existence.

These contrasting reasoning processes are also identified by some as the dialectic of the objective and subjective approaches of human thought. Objectively, we consider that which is outside of ourselves, the subject, without consideration of our response to the object. Subjectively, the human subject observes the object under consideration, taking into account our inner perception, response, and evaluation in order to allow the ontological object to experientially impact our own being. The contrasting approaches of Plato and Aristotle have affected the whole of Western human thought, and have created a perpetual either/or battle of attempting to determine which methodology is more viable, whereas the more acceptable alternative is to accept a both/and dialectic of tensioned balance wherein we recognize that both approaches have their respective spheres of validity.

When the early Christians began to explain the distinctive concept of God that had been revealed in the historic Person of Jesus Christ, the Son of God, they do not seem to have been concerned about the methodological issues of human thinking that had been developed in Greek philosophy. Beginning in the milieu of Jewish culture and religion, when "God sent forth His Son, born of a woman..." (Gal. 4:4), as a male Jewish infant called Immanuel (God with/in us) (cf. Matt. 1:23) who claimed to be the Messiah of the Jews and the Son of God, the Christian followers were hard put to correlate the manner in which God had revealed Himself in the context of Hebrew thought with the prevailing Greek thought structures of the world at that time.

The new covenant literature, the *New Testament*, reveals the contextual difficulties the initial Christians had in sharing their new view of a God-man within the strict monadic monotheistic perspective of first-century Judaism. That contextual difficulty was short-lived, however, for the Roman conquest and genocide of the Jewish peoples between A.D. 66-70 nearly decimated the Hebrew people and for the most part disintegrated the Jewish religion. This near extinction of Jewish culture and theology in which Christian thought had been embryonically rooted meant that from A.D. 70 Christians were forced to share their new perspective of God in the culture and thought of the Greek world. How would they interact with and accommodate the Greek thought of Plato and Aristotle, and the subsequent Gnostic Greek thought that became popular by the second century A.D.? Even within the Johannine literature of the New Testament we begin to observe how Greek concepts such as *Logos* (Word) and *Phos* (light) were utilized to explain Christian thought.

Both Jewish and Christian thinkers attempted to utilize the substantialist metaphysics of Greek philosophical thought in their attempts to explain a monotheistic god. The Jewish philosopher, Philo of Alexandria in Egypt (20 B.C.–A.D. 50), for example, attempted to take such Hebrew concepts of *Yahweh*, *ruach* and *nephesh* and correlate them to the concepts of the metaphysical substances in the Greek "god-box". Even though he was Jewish, he was adept in contemporary Greek language and thought, but was not competent in the Hebrew language. In the third century the philosopher Plotinus of Lycopolis in Egypt (c. A.D. 204-270) revived Platonic thought and contrasted such with the prevalent Gnosticism of his time. The strategic importance of Plotinus and his Neoplatonic thought was his ideological influence upon the Christian thinker, Aurelius Ambrosias (aka Saint Ambrose – A.D. 330-397) of Italy, who became the theological mentor to Augustine.

As Christian thought developed in the West, the trajectory tended to incorporate the Greek process of thinking about the ultimate, the perfect, the singular and supreme god-Being (*cf. Addendum D*). Despite the Apostle Paul's statements, "The wisdom of this world does not know God" (I Cor. 1:20,21); "The wisdom of this world is foolishness before God" (I Cor. 3:18-20); "The natural man cannot understand spiritual things" (I Cor. 2:14); and reference to the "vain philosophies of man" (Col. 2:8), early Christian thinkers attempted to accommodate Greek philosophical categories to explain the Christian God. The historical Self-revelation of God wherein the Son of God, the preexistent (Jn. 1:1,2) "Word became flesh" (Jn. 1:14) "appearing as a man" (Phil. 2:8) presented an anomaly to the singularity (cf. Deut. 6:4) of Jewish monotheism, as well as to the Greek speculation of a mono-Form. When Jesus declared, "I and the Father are one" (Jn. 10:30), the Jews took up stones to kill Him for the obvious blasphemy of claiming to be God. His departing commission to "make disciples … in the name of the Father, the Son, and the Holy Spirit" (Matt. 28:19) served to cement the understanding of the Christian view of a Triune God.

Attempting to explain the Triune God of Christianity in the context of Greek philosophical thought, Christian thinkers found it difficult to articulate the triplicity of divine persons simultaneous with the assertion of monotheistic singularity. A common portrayal of Trinitarian monotheism was to overlay the Trinity of Father, Son, and Holy Spirit on the Greek box of human speculation concerning Ultimate Being. The "God in the box" imagery was trisected to represent a segmented, trichotomous, and tripartite God. The practical effect of such an amalgamative effort of explanation was that the singularity and oneness of the "big box deity" took precedence, and the personal three-ness of Trinitarian understanding was diminished to a cloudy subsidiary mystery.

Telescoping Christian thought out for more than a millennium, we observe two Christian thinkers in particular whose theological premises have predominated and influenced Christian thinking to this very day (*cf. Addendum E*). These two, Aurelius Augustine from North Africa (A.D. 354-430) and Thomas Aquinas from Naples, Italy (A.D. 1225-1274), are regarded by many (both Roman Catholic and

Protestant) as the foremost Christian theologians in the early history of the Church, the "theological doctors" of the Church. What we see in these two thinkers is the adaptation and perpetuation of the methodological procedures of the Greek philosophers, Plato and Aristotle, respectively. Augustine of Hippo employed Plato's *a priori* method of deductive reasoning to explain God, and Thomas of Aquino utilized Aristotle's *a posteriori* method of inductive reasoning to attempt to prove God's existence and composition.

Augustine was trained in philosophy and rhetoric in North Africa. As a young adult he became an adherent of the dualistic Persian religion of Manichaeism for almost a decade. Finding the moral demands of that religion too restrictive, he travelled to Italy and studied under Ambrose, the bishop of Milan, who was a proponent of the thought of the Neoplatonist, Plotinus (noted earlier). Augustine later returned to Africa to become the bishop of Hippo (now Annaba in Algeria).

The Neoplatonic orientation of Augustine's thinking projected the idea of a singular, impersonal and indivisible God. The monotheistic oneness of God (*De Deo Uno*) predominated over the emphasis on the triunity of God (*De Deo Trino*). When Augustine wrote his primary thesis *On the Trinity* (*De Trinitate*), he repeatedly uses the analogy of the human mind as the deductive means of illustrating the divine Trinity, indicating that within the human mind there is memory, thought, and will and these serve as the *vestigia Trinitas*, the psychological vestiges of the Triune God's creation of humanity. So, how does one know that God is a Triune God? Look into the function of your own mind, and you will see the imprint of God. This nouthetic perspective of God's triunity reveals Augustine's philosophical apparatus of rationalism, following in the footsteps of Plato.

Thomas Aquinas, on the other hand, was a Dominican friar in Italy who adopted an Aristotelian philosophical approach to explain God. In his major written work, *Summa Theologica* (treatise or summary of theology), Thomas identifies five proofs of God's existence: (1) Motion or movement requires a mover, therefore God is the "unmoved Mover." (2) Everything must have a cause, with the sole exception that God is the "uncaused Cause." (3) Existence requires previous existence, with the exception that God is the non-contingent Existent Being who created all else that exists. (4) In the gradation of value, the greater creates the lesser, and God is the absolute moral perfection that has created all lesser beings. (5) Purpose requires One who purposes, and God is the intelligent designer who provided purposed objective for all created things. Utilizing the *a posteriori* method of Aristotle, Thomas Aquinas inductively argued backwards from the observed phenomena to a rationalistic perspective of God.

These Augustinian and Thomist presentations of God by some of the foremost theologians of the early Christian church are quite inadequate and misleading. Utilizing the Greek philosophical framework of superlative projections, they only served to formulate conceptions of God that were alien and foreign to how the Father God had gloriously revealed Himself in the Person of Jesus Christ and by the power of the Holy Spirit. In fact, when God is cast as an amalgamation of attributes in a big "Idea Box," such a monadic monotheistic form of god leads to a Unitarian rather than a Trinitarian understanding of God. Such rationalistic constructs whereby human beings attempt to "figure out" the details of God's Being or the procedures of how He functions seem to inevitably lead to some form of idolatrous misrepresentation of God, for idolatry can take the form of a material "golden calf" or a mental construct of a god that is a puny caricature of God. So much of Western Christendom is quite unaware of the extent of its idolatry.

Lest we unfairly indict all the early Christian thinkers as being guilty of appropriating the Greek philosophical structures for explaining God, we should take the time to note a few astute individuals who endeavored to counter the intrusion of classic Greek constructs into Christian thought (*cf. Addendum F*).

In the early part of the fourth century, Arius (A.D. 256-336), a Libyan priest officiating in Alexandria, Egypt, used the natural reasoning of human procreation to advocate, "There was a time when the Son of God was not, ...but at a particular time the Son came into existence out of nothing." This necessarily implied that Jesus was less than eternal God, and denied the orthodox Christian premises of the coequal Persons of the Triune God, that the Son and the Spirit are co-eternal divine Persons and consubstantial with the Father. Such Aristotelian-based reasoning became quite popular, not only in the Alexandrian region but throughout other regions of the church, and the "Arian problem" created much dissent. Roman Emperor Constantine (A.D. 272-337) convened a council of church leaders (A.D. 325) to resolve the dispute that threatened to divide the recently Roman authorized Christian religion. Gathering in Nicea in Bithynia (now Turkey), there were 318 church leaders present. Only five of these were from the Latin Western Church – the other 313 represented the Greek-speaking Eastern Church.

At this initial ecumenical council of the Church, another Alexandrian representative, a young deacon named Athanasius (A.D. 298-373), arose as the foremost proponent of the Trinitarian monotheism that was distinctive to Christian faith. Called by some "the black dwarf," Athanasius was forensically adept at countering the Greek-based monadic view of God expressed by Arius and his supporters, and defending the belief that Jesus, the Son of God, was consubstantial, or of the "same being" with the Father. The Nicene Creed, drafted and accepted by all but three attendees of the Council of Nicea, used the word *homoousion* meaning "same being" to state that the Lord Jesus Christ was ὁμοούσιον τῷ Πατρί, "the same being as the Father," i.e. of co-equal deity with God the Father. Athanasius won the day in helping to formulate the orthodox Christian assertion of the co-essential divinity of God the Father and God the Son.

It was not until the second ecumenical council of the Church convened in Constantinople in A.D. 381 that the issue of the deity of the Holy Spirit was explicitly expressed, and the original Nicene Creed was enhanced and expanded to state that "the Holy Ghost is the Lord and Giver of life, who proceeds from the Father, and who with the Father and Son together is worshipped and glorified." This is the version of the Nicene Creed most used in the church today. As the third Person of the Godhead, the Holy Spirit was identified as divine "Lord" and the "Giver of life" (cf. I Cor. 15:45) and worthy of being "worshipped and glorified" as God.

The Council of Constantinople was chaired by one of the three influential Church leaders who are known as "the Cappadocian Fathers," referring to the region of Cappadocia in central Turkey from whence they hailed. Basil the Great (A.D. 329-379), who served as the bishop of Caesarea Mazacca in Cappadocia, died two years prior to this second council, but his younger brother, Gregory of Nyssa (A.D. 335-395), was in attendance, and their close friend, Gregory of Nazianzus (A.D. 329-389), who had recently become the Archbishop of Constantinople, served to lead the council along with Theodosius, the Roman Emperor. The Council of Constantinople was attended by only 150 leaders of the Eastern Greek-speaking church, and there were no representatives from the Western Latin Church present.

What is known as the "Cappadocian Settlement" formulated the Trinitarian explanation that God exists as One Being (*mia ousia*) in three Persons (*treis hypostaseis*). The three Persons are not three independent, autonomous beings, but within the singular Being of God they function in perfect interpersonal communion or fellowship, and this internal relational interaction comprises the essential Being (*ousia*) of the Triune God. The three Persons of the One Being of God function in *perichoresis,* whereby they are "in one another," in a unique coinherence and mutual interpenetration that disallows all charges of tritheism (three gods), as well as the modalism that would consider the threeness to be merely three modes of expression of a single god. In this manner the unity and diversity of the Godhead is preserved, and the Greek philosophical structure of the substantialist composition of the "being" of the singular Ideal is overcome by the distinctively personal and relational Being of God as revealed in the incarnate Son. The extended emphasis of the Cappadocian Fathers on the process of *Theosis* explained how their Trinitarian emphasis on God's Being could be brought into the personal experience of Christians as the loving interrelations of Father, Son, and Holy Spirit could be perichoretically functional in the holy living of individual Christians as they communed and fellowshipped with the Triune God and with one another in the Body of Christ, the Church.

It should be remembered that Athanasius and
the Cappadocian trio were part of the Eastern Greek-
speaking Church, and in the ensuing years and centuries
of Christian history the Western Latin Church would
predominate, with the intricacies of the Greek words
and phrases used to express Trinitarian thought being
obscured in translation or swallowed up by scholastic
speculation. Augustine, for example, spoke and wrote in
Latin, with a less than competent grasp of the Greek
language, and admitted that he could not comprehend
the Trinitarian language of the Cappadocian statements
at the Council of Constantinople. In his treatise *De
Trinitate*, Augustine writes of the Cappadocians,

> "They use the word *hypostasis*; but they intend to put a
> difference, I know not what, between *ousia* and
> *hypostasis*; so that most of those who treat these things in
> the Greek language are accustomed to say, *mian ousian,
> tres hypostases*, or (as we say), in Latin, one essence,
> three substances (*unam essentiam, tres substantias*)."

Failing to comprehend the Greek Trinitarian words,
Augustine reverts to the Latin vocabulary that casts the
explanation of God back into the substantive
metaphysics of Greek philosophy as multiple substances
in a singular essence.

The theological paradigm employed by the Cappadocians that resisted the philosophical presuppositions of the early Greek philosophers would soon fade away in a return to Hellenized thinking (as evidenced in Augustine and Aquinas). The history of Western theological thinking has thus been characterized by more of a philosophical methodology than by a divinely initiated revelatory approach (*oikonomia*) that explains the Triune God via the incarnation and the redemptive sacrifice of the Son, Jesus Christ. The classical methodology of the Greek philosophers has been utilized to construct the foundational structures of Christian theology, and this approach has been labeled "Classical Theism." It has also been called "natural theology," based on the natural reasoning of human thought, rather than the "revealed theology" of God's revelation of Himself.

Greek philosophical thought hypothesized the "being" (*ousia*) of the singular ultimate Form-figure that was regarded as the all-encompassing ideal entity that pervades and shapes all things. This ideological abstraction was logically conceived as having the attributes of singularity, simplicity, indivisibility, immutability, impassibility, inscrutability, etc. As such, it was regarded as impersonal and (for the most part) a-relational, incapable of any diversity of personhood, and therefore preemptively disqualifying any proper Trinitarian concept of God.

What we need in Christian thought, even after the accumulated discussion of many centuries, is a more adequate and proper awareness of the Triune God. We must go beyond the "Big Box" of speculative superlatives, negative denials, and omni-attributes whereby human logic has attempted to formulate the necessary logical Being of the Absolute One. This must give way to a distinctively Christian perspective of God in the manner that He has revealed Himself as Father, Son, and Holy Spirit, relationally interacting in LOVE, and thereby allowing us to articulate a legitimate Christian Trinitarian monotheism.

The Christian understanding of the Trinity of God is more than a numerical denominating and particularizing of the "god in the box." The sterility of the "numerical Trinity" of Christianized philosophy must be replaced by the awareness of the "relational

Trinity" wherein we recognize that the very Being of God is intrinsically and dynamically constituted and energized by the eternal loving relationships of the Father, Son, and Holy Spirit within the Triune God, who has historically revealed Himself in space and time in the divine-human mediator, Jesus Christ, and the empowering presence of the Holy Spirit.

Christians must take into account that the historic Person of Jesus declared, "I and the Father are one" (Jn. 10:30). This was an assertion of His essential and relational oneness with God the Father, and not just a statement of common intent and purpose. Jesus' repetitive "I AM" statements (cf. Jn. 11:25; 14:6; 15:1,5) were understood to be identification with the "I AM" Self-naming of God the Father (Exod. 3:14). Jesus explained to Philip, "He who has seen Me has seen the Father. ... Do you not believe that I am in the Father, and the Father is in Me? (Jn. 14:9,10), implying that there is an indwelling, interpenetrative, coinherent, or perichoretic oneness of Father and Son. Matthew records Jesus' statement, "No one knows the Son except the Father; nor does anyone know the Father except the Son, and anyone to whom the Son wills to reveal Him"

(Matthew 11:27). This accords with John's comment, "No one has seen God at any time, the only begotten … He has explained (exegeted) Him" (John 1:18). Since Jesus IS the revelation of God, there is no legitimate Christian conception of God apart from the historical and experiential Jesus. God can only be properly understood via the Self-revelation of Himself in the Son, Jesus Christ.

Instead of the *substantive* metaphysics of Greek philosophy, Christian theology must begin with a *relational* metaphysics of the ontological relations of the Persons of the Triune God. The divine *ousia* (Being) is not an abstract ultimate substance conceptualized via the unaided human reasoning of philosophical projections. Rather, the Being (*ousia*) of God is discovered in the revealed relationality of the multiplicity of divine Persons as they dynamically interact with diversity in unity, sharing the character of divine love (*agape*) that always seeks the highest good of the other and thus the whole. In fact, John's statement, "God is love" (I Jn. 4:8,16) can only be viable if we accept the Triune God. Love is relational. Love is other-oriented. If there were not multiple "others" in the Being of the tri-personal God, then love would be but an empty abstraction or an ethereal emotive affectation, and could not legitimately be used of God's constitutive Being.

The Christian contention is that the essential relational *ousia* (Being) of God necessitates His being a multi-personal God who serves as the divine dynamic of all loving interpersonal relationships. There never was a time when God was not engaged in the interpersonal relationality of His multi-personal singularity of Being. The essential Being of God can only be described in terms of the loving relationality of the Persons of the Father, Son, and Holy Spirit. The relationality of the divine Persons is the supreme ontological premise of a Christian understanding of God. It is imperative for Christians to understand the divine Persons in relationship among themselves constitute the *ousia* (Being) of God. God is an inter-relational Being. Relationality and mutuality are at the heart of God's Being. Christians must maintain an onto-relational Trinitarian theological perspective.

In order to properly explain the God who revealed Himself in Jesus Christ, Christians must obviously go beyond the static "God in the box" image of the Greeks, wherein the *ousia* of supreme "being" is comprised of abstracted substances of a philosophical ideal. But we must avoid taking that metaphysical speculation of a "God in the box" and attempting to overlay a trisected perspective of a tripartite God on top of the god-box image (*cf. Addendum G*). This seems to have been the tendency of so much of Western Christian theological explanation. Preoccupied with the numerical dilemma of how to make the threeness of the Godhead fit into the oneness of God's "Being," many theologians have superimposed three compartments over the abstract god-box. This is a most inadequate representation of God's triunity, which may avoid the accusations of tri-theism (that there are three gods) but easily degenerates into a monadic monotheism wherein God's multiplicity is regarded as but three aspects or modes of expressing Himself. This form of non-trinitarian modalism was propounded by Sabellius in the 3rd century and rejected as heretical by the church at large, though remnants of such thought have arisen in the history of theological thought.

A variation of such modalism can be seen in the explanation of the sequential, successive function of the three divine Persons. Some have attempted to explain that the Father-mode of God was operative in the Old Testament, the Son-mode of God was operative in the gospels, and the Spirit-mode of God is predominantly operative within the book of Acts through Revelation. This misguided, modalistic explanation tends to cast the three Persons of God into a relay team, where one person passes the baton to the next divine "runner," and it fails to retain the relational unity of the Trinity.

Another misconception and misrepresentation (*cf. Addendum H*) that seems to prevail in Western Christian thought also retains the abstracted "god in the box" idea of Greek philosophical thought, but projects Father, Son and Holy Spirit as the "front men" for the invisible god-figure. The BIG god, the real god, the authoritative god-figure resides in the inner sanctum of the heavenly control room – "command central." Hidden behind the scenes, He sets the administrative agenda and "calls the shots," employing His sovereign power to implement His determinations. Many refer to Him as "the Big Man upstairs," or "the divine Judge in the sky."

Meanwhile, the three persons of the Godhead provide a "united front" for God. They are engaged in doing the bidding of the "Boss Man" by implementing the agenda of the enigmatic divine CEO. They serve as God's political action committee. To use a sports analogy, they serve as God's "offensive line." This imagery may sound bizarre, but so many Christian people seem to inadvertently have the idea that behind the persons and actions of Father, Son and Holy Spirit, there exists an austere authority in the backroom of the distant heavenlies who controls the joy-stick of divine activity, particularly for the Son and the Spirit.

It is of utmost importance that Christian thought pertaining to the Triune God be focused on the personal relations of the three Persons of the One God – the relational Being of God. We proceed, then, to consider an admittedly inadequate two-dimensional illustration of the dynamic relational interaction of the three Persons of the Triune God (cf. *Addendum I)* that will serve to demonstrate the radical difference between the philosophical projections of human philosophy and the Self-revealed *ousia* (Being) of God, constituted by the personal relations of the three Persons of the Father,

Son, and Holy Spirit. The circles representing the three divine Persons overlap with one another, representing their intrinsic *enousia* of "being" in relation with one another and the perichoretic function (*perichoresis*: *peri*=around, *chora*=space) whereby they exist and move around in the same space to the extent that one cannot exist or function apart from the others – a mutual indwelling, coinherence and interpenetrative oneness. The triple concentric circle connecting the circular representations of the three persons is intended to illustrate the perfect circle of love that exists as the character of divine love flows in the personal relationships between them. Every human analogy and illustration falls short as we attempt to explain the triune God, but this is without a doubt better than the "god in the box" illustration of common human reasoning.

Oikonomia

What we have attempted to explain is that to develop a distinctively Christian *theologia*, a proper Christian consideration of the Triune God, the Trinity, the three persons of Father, Son and Holy Spirit constituting the relational Being of the One monotheistic God – such must be informed by, and founded upon, the *oikonomia*, i.e. the awareness of and interpretation of the historical working of God in the only begotten Son, Jesus Christ, and by the work of the Holy Spirit. God can only properly be known by human beings to the extent and in the manner in which He has revealed Himself via the Son and the Spirit. On the basis of the historical revelation of God from the incarnation of the Son Jesus Christ to the Pentecostal outpouring of the Holy Spirit, we have the means by which to form and articulate a Christian *theologia* of God that explains the personally relational Trinity – a concept of God unlike any other in the history of human considerations of God – because it is based on Divine revelation and not merely on human speculation.

In previous writings I have stated, "God *does* what He *does*, because He *is* who He *is*." That remains true! God's work, His doing, is predicated on His Being. *Oikonomia* stems from, and is a result of *theologia*. But there is also the sense that we can only know who He *is* (*theologia*) on the basis of what He has chosen to *do* in His Self-revelation of Himself within the action of the Son and the Spirit in human history (*oikonomia*). We know by what He has done that He is a loving relational Being, and not just a logical abstraction. These categories are mutually beneficial to the understanding of the other.

In the introductory explanation of the meaning of the Greek word *oikonomia*, we noted that the word is derived from two Greek words: *oikos* = household; and *nomos* = law. It pertains to the laws or rules of the household, by which the household is managed and administrated. Since it was the steward of the house who was responsible for such management, the word *oikonomia* is also sometimes translated as "stewardship," or even as the "dispensation" of how the household is managed. Some theological camps have taken the word "dispensation" and developed elaborate schemes of how God is alleged to manage His affairs in various "dispensations" of time (ex. Dispensationalism), but that is not the focus of this study.

Our objective is to explain that the relational Triune God, Father, Son, and Holy Spirit, functioned purposefully and administratively in every phase and feature of His conjoined operation throughout human history. We want to observe the triadic action of God throughout the whole of God's economy, and the grace-action by which the Triune God has accomplished His eternal administrative purpose and plan for humanity.

The diagram (*cf. Addendum J*) we will be using is a simple time-line drawing that I have used in previous teaching. This diagram focuses on the earthly life of Jesus Christ, for such is certainly the spotlight of God's Self-revelation of Himself. God specifically revealed Himself via the incarnational advent and subordinated actions of the Son, Jesus Christ.

But we want to note that God's administrative *oikonomia* – His complete functional work energized by His own grace – has always, eternally, preexistently, prior to the existence of the earth and humanity, been the expression and work of the three Persons of the triune Godhead simultaneously, and never in separated detachment or independence from one another.

In creation we note, "In the beginning *God* created the heavens and the earth" (Gen. 1:1), and then in the very next verse, Gen. 1:2, "the *Spirit of God* was moving over the surface of the waters." Then in John 1:1,14 we read, "In the beginning was the *Word*, ...and the Word was God. The Word was made flesh." The Word, the Son of God, *Jesus*, was "in the beginning with God, and all things came into being by Him, and apart from Him nothing came into being that has come into being" (John 1:3). Hebrews 11:3 states that "the worlds were prepared by the Word (*Logos)* of God." What do we see here? That the relational Triune God was operative even in the creative commencement of our physical world.

Now, more specifically, we shall note that the incarnation of the Son into human history was accomplished by the action of the three Persons of the Godhead. John 3:16 reads, "God so loved the world that

He gave His only begotten Son..." In Gal. 4:4 Paul explains, "When the fullness of time came, *God* (the Father) sent forth His *Son*, born of a woman," (and he goes on in 4:6 to refer to "the *Spirit* of the Son"). The Son of God was obviously involved, for He "emptied Himself, taking the form of a bondservant, being made in the likeness of men" (Phil. 2:7). "The Word was made flesh" (John 1:14); He was "revealed in the flesh" (I Tim. 3:16). The Spirit of God was also involved in the incarnation of Jesus for we are told that Mary "was found to be with child by the *Holy Spirit*" (Matt. 1:18,20; cf. Lk. 1:35). The entire Trinity was operative in the incarnation of Jesus Christ.

Just a brief sidenote here: the Son of God became the eternal God-man. The Son, one of the Persons of the Triune Godhead, became both divine and human simultaneously, without either category of "being" (divine being or human being) being diminished, tarnished, or neglected. At the Council of Chalcedon in A.D. 451 the Christian thinkers of the time attempted to articulate this union of deity and humanity in the single person of Jesus Christ by referring to the "hypostatic union" of the God-man mediator between God and man (cf. I Tim. 2:5). That explanation has persisted in the Western Church to this very day. Jesus is forever the Son of God; Jesus is forever the God-man. Jesus was born as a man (Phil. 2:7); He died as a man (Matt. 20:18,19); He rose as a man (Matt. 17:9); he ascended as a man (Jn. 6:62); He was enthroned as a man (Matt. 26:64); He returned to the glory of His Father as a man (Matt. 25:31); and He reigns forever as the God-man (Lk. 1:31-33). He never ceases to be the God-man mediator between God and mankind.

Throughout the life of Jesus Christ on earth we continue to see the *oikonomia* action of the three Persons of the Trinity. When Jesus was baptized by John the Baptist in the Jordan River (Mk. 1:9-11; Matt. 3:16,17; Lk. 3:22) the narrative reads, "a voice came out of the heavens: 'Thou are My (*the Father*) beloved *Son*, in Thee I am well pleased," and the *Spirit* in the form of a dove descended upon Him and compelled Him to go into the wilderness to be tempted and then to commence His public ministry.

Though distinctively the Son of God, Jesus lived, moved and worked inseparably from the functioning of

the Father and the Spirit. He was "full of the *Holy Spirit*"
(Lk. 4:1), was led by the *Spirit* (Lk. 4:1), and operated
"in the power of the *Spirit*" (Lk. 1:14). He "cast out
demons by the *Spirit of God*" (Matt. 12:28). Jesus
repeatedly explained that He did nothing singularly or
independently by Himself, but only what He saw the
Father doing and what the *Father* taught Him (cf. John
5:19,30; 8:28); what was "pleasing to the *Father*" (Jn.
8:29). "The *Father* abiding in Me does His works" (Jn.
14:10). That is why Jesus could say, "If you have seen
Me, you have seen the *Father*" (Jn. 14:9-11). The Triune
God was working in everything Jesus did, even though
conceptually it was the Son who was visually apparent
to those who observed His life as the *prima facie*
personage of the triune God.

When Jesus was crucified on the cross of Calvary
it was the distinct action of the Son being crucified, for
God cannot die. An early church writer, Tertullian (A.D.
160-225), cautioned against *patripassionism*, the idea
that God the Father suffered and died on the cross, and
the need to note that the Son of God, the God-man, died
on the cross. Nonetheless, it is necessary to note that
the totality of the Trinity was involved in the crucifixion

event. The Son was never separated or detached from the action of the Father and the Spirit. Writing to the Colossian Christians, Paul explained that God the Father "cancelled out the certificate of debt" against humanity, "having nailed it to the cross" (Colossians 2:14). And in the letter to the Hebrews we are informed, "*Christ*, through the eternal *Spirit*, offered Himself without blemish to *God*" (Heb. 9:14). These verses attest to the action of the entire triune God in Jesus' death on the cross.

Then, in the resurrection of Jesus Christ from the dead, we continue to see the full operation of the Triune God. Peter explained "this *Jesus*, *God* (the Father) raised up" (Acts 2:32; 3:15); "*God* raised Him up on the third day" (Acts 10:40). But the Son was active in His own resurrection also: He told the Jewish leaders, "Destroy this temple (of His own body), and in three days I will raise it up again" (John 2:19,21). "I lay down My life, that I may take it up again" (Jn. 10:17,18) in the resurrection. The divine Spirit was also at work in the resurrection, for in Peter's first epistle, he writes that "*Christ* ... was put to death in the flesh, but made alive in the *spirit*" (I Pet. 3:18), and Paul mentions "the *Spirit* of

Him who raised Jesus from the dead" (Rom. 8:11). All three Persons of the Triune God were operative in the resurrection of Jesus.

Then in the exaltation of Jesus by the subsequent ascension of Jesus to the heavenly presence of God (Acts 1:9-11), the Son was instrumentally involved, for Jesus told Mary, "Do not cling to Me; I have not yet ascended to the Father" (Jn. 20:17). The apostle Peter later explained that "Christ Jesus is at the right hand of God, having gone into heaven after angels and authorities and power had been subjected to Him" (I Peter 3:22), and He was "made Lord of all" (Acts 10:36). In Acts 5:31 in Peter's preaching, he refers to "the One (Jesus Christ) whom God (the Father) exalted to His right hand." To the Philippians, Paul wrote, "God (the Father) highly exalted Him (Jesus)...that every tongue should confess that Jesus Christ is Lord" (Phil. 2:11). And then in that fantastic passage in Ephesians 1 we read of the "surpassing greatness of *God's* power ...which He brought about in *Christ*, when He raised Him from the dead, and seated Him at His right hand in the heavenly places, far above all rule and authority and power and dominion, and every name that is named, not only in this age, but also in the age to come" (Eph. 1:19-21). The Trinity was involved in the ascension of Jesus.

To complete this survey of the *oikonomia* activity of the three Persons of the Trinity in the historic life and work of Jesus on earth, we must note that 50 days after the Passover when Jesus, the Lamb of God, was slain, came the Jewish Pentecost festival, as recorded in Acts chapter two. Are we still speaking of the life and work of Jesus Christ after His ascension to the Father in heaven? Yes, without a doubt! So much of the church has often missed the fact that the Pentecostal outpouring was the blessing of the outpouring of the *Spirit* of the resurrected and ascended *Jesus Christ.* The living Lord Jesus Christ returns to His disciples in Spirit-form on Pentecost. Those who miss this point miss the dynamic of the Christian life! What a tragic slight in so much Christian teaching!

This is what Jesus was attempting to convey to His disciples in the Upper Room discourse of John 14:16-17: "I will ask the Father, and He will give you another Helper (or Comforter, or Encourager, or Advocate – another who will "come to your aid"); that

He (not "it" – masculine personal pronoun – not just a spirit-force) may be with you forever; that is the Spirit of truth, whom the world cannot receive, because it does not behold Him or know Him, but you know Him because He abides (resides) with you, and will be in you. I will not leave you as orphans; I will come to you" (John 14:16-18). Take notice of these pertinent points:

•...The Son of God promises to ask God the Father to give to the disciples (and that extends to all the disciples of Christ in every age) the Spirit ...

•... another Helper/Comforter/Encourager/ Advocate. The Greek word is *parakletos*. You may have heard some preachers refer to the Holy Spirit as the Paraclete. Paraclete refers to someone who comes alongside to assist, and that is why it is sometimes translated "Counselor." In the legal venue it is translated as an "Advocate." The living Lord Jesus is identified with this very word (*parakletos*) in I John 2:1 where John writes, "If anyone sins, we have an Advocate with the Father, Jesus Christ the righteous." It is also used of Barnabas when he was called the "Son of Encouragement or Consolation"

(Acts 4:36). The point being made here is that this word, parakletos, is used of Jesus Christ.

•...Jesus then promises to send "another" One to assist, comfort and aid when He has departed physically. There are two Greek words for "another." There is the word *heteros*, which means "another of a different kind." We use the word in reference to a *hetero*sexual – one who enters into a sexual relationship with another person of a different kind, a different gender, a male and a female. That is *heteros*. But that is NOT the word that Jesus uses when He promises His disciples to send "another" Comforter. Instead, Jesus uses the Greek word *allos* (instead of *heteros*), meaning "another of the same kind." This "another" one who is to come to the aid and assistance of the disciples is not just "another of the same kind" because He, too, is divine; but because we are dealing with the divine Trinity, this "another of the same kind" is "another of the same kind" because He is One with Me; He is the same One; it will be ME in Spirit-form, Who is going to come to you, and "abide" (take up residence and make His home with you), and be IN you. .... Forever!

By the way, a scriptural contrast between the Greek words *heteros* and *allos* can be viewed in Paul's epistle to the Galatians: "I am amazed that you are so quickly deserting Him who called you by the grace of Christ, for *another* (or a different – Greek word *heteros*) gospel; which is not really another (*allos* – of the same kind of gospel); there are those who want to distort the gospel of Christ..." (1:6,7). They are telling you things that are not gospel at all!

•.... Jesus caps off his comments to the disciples saying, "In My going away, accepting imminent death at the hands of the Jewish leaders and the Roman officials, accepting an underserved death for the sins of mankind, I will not leave you as abandoned orphans running to and fro looking for someone to attach themselves to, ...I will come to you." Notice the first person pronoun: "**I**" will come to you. **I**, Jesus, will come in Spirit-form. Jesus was promising that He would come to aid and assist His disciples in the form of the Spirit, and this was historically enacted at Pentecost.

Jesus reiterates this to the disciples in John 16:13-15 in slightly different words, "When He, the Spirit of truth, comes, He will guide you into all the truth; for He will not speak on His own initiative, but whatever He hears, He will speak; and He will disclose to you what is to come. He shall glorify Me; for He shall take of Mine, and shall disclose it to you. All things that the Father has are Mine; therefore I said, that He takes of Mine, and will disclose it to you." These words only make sense when we have a perspective of the interactive involvement of the Triune God.

We move on to clarify the importance of what occurred at Pentecost in the outpouring of the Spirit of Christ, allowing the living Lord Jesus to live within His disciples by the Spirit.

There is a very important statement in Paul's chapter on resurrection in I Cor. 15. Quoting Gen. 2:7, Paul writes "it is written, 'The first man, Adam, became a living soul." But then Paul goes on to say, "The last Adam (obviously referring to Jesus Christ, especially if we remember the contrast that Paul drew in Romans chapter 5) became life-giving Spirit." I think this is a pivotal statement for understanding the ongoing spiritual life of Jesus in Christian peoples. I think that Paul means that the resurrected and living Jesus Christ became, and was manifested as, the life-giving Spirit, in order to dwell within us and be our life. This serves as the necessary amplification of what Jesus told His disciples in the Upper Room prior to His crucifixion.

We turn now to II Corinthians 3:17,18, keeping in mind that we are observing how the risen and ascended Lord Jesus is one with, and manifested by, the Spirit from Pentecost onwards: "Now the Lord (who is the Lord? Look at 4:5 – "we preach Christ Jesus as Lord.") … "Now the Lord (Jesus Christ) is the Spirit; and where the Spirit of the Lord (Jesus Christ) is, there is liberty. But we all, with unveiled face beholding as in a mirror the glory of the Lord, are being transformed in the same image from glory to glory, just as from the Lord (Jesus Christ), the Spirit." Is it not evident that Paul is equating the Lord Jesus Christ and the Spirit? I do not see how we can come to any other conclusion if we understand the Triune God, the distinctive three-in-oneness of the Christian understanding of God.

Throughout the history of Christian teaching there have been so many teachers and groups who have failed to grasp and understand what we might call "the Pneumatic Christ," and how the resurrected and living Lord Jesus came in Spirit-form to draw persons to Himself from Pentecost onwards and to be the dynamic of the Church of Jesus Christ.

The relational dynamic of the three Persons of the Godhead have often been obscured and misrepresented. The relational oneness of the God and Father and God the Son has been misunderstood, and the relational oneness of God the Son and God the Spirit has been obscured.

I share with you a true story about a man whom I knew personally. He has since graduated to glory – in 2007. He was a Scottish pastor who volunteered to be a chaplain to the British troops in WWII. Toward the end of the Second World War during a battle in northern Italy, a young British soldier was mortally wounded, and as he lay there dying, he asked the chaplain what might have seemed like a strange question from a dying man. He asked, "Chaplain, Is God the same as Jesus?"

Why do you think a dying young man might have asked that question? This young dying soldier was a Christian. He knew that Christians believe in the Trinity, and He did. He knew Christians believe that Jesus is God, and He did. But there is one area where there has been a breakdown in Christian teaching in our Western churches. We have given the mistaken impression that God the Father is a strict Judge who demands that the penalty of death be paid for sin. And conversely we have portrayed Jesus, the Son of God, as the One who is full of compassionate LOVE, who was willing to volunteer as the substitute who would take the wrath and judgment of the Father on our behalf, by being put to death on the execution instrument of the cross. What is the problem with that differentiation? It creates a polarized dichotomy, a bifurcation, between the thought and attitude of God the Father and God the Son, which in effect violates and destroys the Christian concept of the Trinity. Father, Son, and Holy Spirit are always ONE in their LOVE for mankind. They are always *for* us, and *not against* us! Their greatest desire is to draw us into participation in their perfect interrelations of LOVE.

How sad that some Christians today think that God the Father and God the Son are of a "divided mind." The Father is *against* us; the Son is *for* us. One young boy in Sunday School explained: "I don't like that Big God, the Father God – He's mean! But Jesus, He loves me, and I like Him!" This kind of thinking comes from our failure to explain that God the Father, God the Son, and God the Holy Spirit have a *perfect relationship* of loving oneness – oneness of Being, oneness of mind and attitude – totally together in their LOVE, and in their desire to draw us into participation with them in the divine fellowship of the Trinity.

So, when the dying soldier asked, "Is God the same as Jesus?" the chaplain replied, "Yes son, the entirety of the Godhead is of the same mind and character as Jesus – loving … forgiving … willing to sacrifice everything for us, and desiring an eternal relationship with us. Jesus the Savior, was (as is) the Self-revelation of the Triune God, and when you see the loving heart of Jesus, you have seen GOD." Remember the words of Jesus to Philip just before He was crucified? He said, "He who has seen Me (Jesus), has seen the Father" (John 14:9). "He who knows Me

(Jesus), knows the Father." God, in all three persons, is the same as Jesus. They have the same divine character and intent!

The name of that chaplain was Thomas Forsyth Torrance, who was the chair of the dogmatic theology department at the University of Edinburgh, Scotland when I studied there in the late 1960s, and he went on to become known as the foremost Scottish theologian of all time.

The misunderstanding of the relational oneness of God the Son and God the Spirit can be illustrated by my sharing another anecdotal story.

I share with you a conversation I had with a friend with whom I had numerous theological conversations. In fact I spent hundreds of hours visiting with him on the telephone. His name was James Seward, and he too has now graduated to glory. He had read and meticulously combed through almost everything that I had written.

On more than one occasion he said to me, "Jim Fowler, you seem to be referring to the indwelling Christ, the living Lord Jesus within you, and the Holy Spirit in you, as if they were the same thing, the same reality. You seem to be using "Christ in you" as if it were equivalent to the Holy Spirit in our spirit."

I replied, "Yes... and your point is ..."

Jim Seward continued, "I am concerned that you are not preserving the *distinction* between the Son and the Spirit; that you are not maintaining the "*threeness*" of the Godhead."

I replied, "Huummm...

"I, on the other hand, am concerned that you (Jim Seward) are not preserving the *unity* of the Son and the Holy Spirit; that you are not maintaining the functional "*Oneness*" of the Godhead." "You seem to want to emphasize that the Son and the Spirit are separate individuals, or separate gods almost."

"As I understand it, the Son and the Spirit are NOT different *individuals,* even though they are distinct *Persons.* The Son and the Spirit are NOT *separate,* but they do have *distinct* function. The Son and the Spirit are *united* in their essential Being as God. It is quite legitimate to refer to one Person of the Godhead in the same manner as the other two, for they are never present or functioning without the other divine Persons.

"So, you are correct, Mr. Seward, in your observations that when I make reference to the living "Christ," for example, in the phrase "Christ in you, the hope of glory" (Col. 1:27), I am thinking of the entirety of the Triune God, Father, Son, and HS, the indwelling of the tri-personal God within one's spirit. I have no intention or desire to separate the Son from the Father or the Spirit. When I refer to Jesus Christ, it is always in the context of Trinity. The Father, the Son and the Spirit are three Persons in ONE relational Being. Reference to the Persons of the Godhead can be made inter-changeably because they are coinherent and consubstantial within the singular, relational divine Being. They are capable of distinction, but not separation. They do not act independently, but always conjunctively and simultaneously.

That is why we take the time to note that in every event of the *oikonomia* of God's work in the historic life of Jesus Christ, the three Persons of the Trinity were functioning simultaneously and interrelationally in every event of Jesus' historic life. Yes, the physical Jesus was the *prima facie* personage who appeared empirically to those around Him, but the Father and the Spirit were present and functioning with Him in every event of the triune God's Self-revelation. Where one of the Persons of the Godhead is, they all are! Where one is acting, they all are present in the action. In the perichoretic interrelations of the Trinity, Father, Son, and Holy Spirit mutually interpenetrate, coinhere, and move around in the space of the other (*peri*=around; *chora*=space). The triune Persons are *enousia* – their "being" is in relation with one another.

The revelation of the Triune God in the entirety of the life and work of Jesus Christ serves to inform our *theologia*, our human considerations of how the Christian perspective of God is uniquely that of a relationally Triune God, and our relational Triune theology in a mutually reciprocal interaction informs our study and interpretation of the gospel record in the new covenant literature of the New Testament. *Theologia* and *oikonomia* are mutually dependent and reciprocally interactive categories.

We have noted that the triune God made Himself known historically in the *oikonomia* as a relational God, but must proceed to explain that God continues in every age to act upon relational human beings by His grace in order to effect a personal and relational *koinonia* with every individual. Apart from accepting and entering experientially into the onto-relationalism of the triune God, we do not know God! Christ-ones, Christians, are made sharers in the very life of the triune God, "partakers of the divine nature" (II Pet. 1:4).

Koinonia

When we introduced the three Greek words that we are using in this study, we noted that *koinonia* is derived from the Greek word *koine*, meaning "common," and in the context of our study on the Triune God it pertains to the common union that Christians have with the Father, Son, and Holy Spirit, and with one another in the Christian community. The word is often translated into English as "fellowship, partnership, sharing, participation, or even communion." It is the word used in I John 1:3, indicating, "our *fellowship* is with the Father, and with His Son, Jesus Christ." To the Corinthians, Paul explained, "God is faithful, through whom you were called into *fellowship* with His Son, Jesus Christ our Lord" (I Cor. 1:9). Later Paul wrote, "The grace of the Lord Jesus Christ, and the love of God, and the *fellowship* of the Holy Spirit, be with you all" (II Cor. 13:14). The entirety of the Trinity is involved in the experiential *koinonia* with human individuals that we are referring to.

Christians are meant to have a unique, subjective, and personal participatory experience with the divine Trinity. Though this has often been relegated to a rather subdued emphasis in Western Christian thought, often "swept under the rug" so to speak, this is most unfortunate, for this personal relationship and experience with the Triune God is the ultimate objective of God in creating mankind, and the foremost fulfillment and satisfaction for every individual. The "good news" of the gospel is not just an historic salvation purchased by Jesus the Savior on the cross, in order to get human beings "off the hook" for their sin; get their slate wiped clean; and grant them a "ticket to heaven." No – God's Self-giving redemption and salvation was for the purpose of giving Himself, Father, Son and Holy Spirit to allow us to participate and fellowship with Him in the perfect interactions of Triune LOVE (cf. *Addendum K*).

The Eastern Orthodox churches – the Greek-speaking churches – have understood this since the very first days of the Church. That is why they have, and do to this day, define salvation as *Theosis*, the process of being in-Godded, of being enlivened and enlightened with the very life and light of the Triune God, whereby the very energies of God-ness are applied to Christian believers. The Triune God is brought into human beings, and human individuals are joined with God in spiritual union. The Western Church, originally the Latin speaking church, has always been leery of that Greek word *Theosis*, thinking that it meant the deification or divinization of human beings, but the Greek-speaking church has always tried to explain that they do not mean that human beings become the essence of God, but that human beings are meant to participate relationally in the energies, the working, the expression of the character of God – Father, Son, and Holy Spirit.

Even in the initiatory act of Christian baptism the words of Jesus are almost always cited, that we are being baptized "in the name of the *Father* and the *Son* and the *Holy Spirit*" (Matt. 25:19). The one being baptized, and those observing the ceremony, are encouraged to recognize that the one being overwhelmed by the water (whatever the mode) is illustrating the action of the Triune God, Father, Son and Holy Spirit, overwhelming the human spirit with His presence. Paul explained that "by one Spirit we were all baptized into one body, whether Jews or Greeks, whether slaves or free, and we were all made to drink of one Spirit" (I Cor. 12:13), whereby we fellowship and participate with and in the Triune God.

All that God does in our Christian lives is by the dynamic participation and sharing of His Trinitarian grace. "The God of all grace ...perfects, confirms, strengthens and establishes us" (I Pet. 5:10). Paul admits straight-forwardly, "By the grace of God, I am what I am" (I Cor. 15:10). God's grace is the dynamic of His Triune activity in our lives. "The grace of our Lord Jesus Christ" (II Cor. 13:14) by the "Spirit of grace" (Heb. 10:29) operates with and in the spirits of Christian persons (cf. Gal. 6:18).

God's love activity in and through us is a Triune expression of divine love. "The love of *God* has been poured out within our hearts through the *Holy Spirit* who He has given to us" (Rom. 5:5), and "nothing is able to separate us from the love of *Christ* (8:35) or the love of God which is in Christ Jesus" (Rom. 8:39). The "love of *Christ* constrains us, compels us, and controls us" (II Cor. 5:14) to participate in "the love of the *Spirit*" (Rom. 15:30). The *agape* love of God is the love of the Father,

Son, and Holy Spirit, intended to be expressed in our human behavior.

Within (*cf. Addendum L*) the concentric circles representing the constitution of a human being comprised of spiritual, psychological, and bodily function (cf. I Thess. 5:23; Heb. 4:12), we have placed the diagram of the relational Being of the Triune God, Father, Son, and Holy Spirit. Since the human person is a derivative being, who does not have independent function like God, there must be an indwelling spirit-being who provides spiritual being, nature, identity, and destiny to the individual. There is no innate divinity in a human person, no "spark of the divine" in every man, not even a "God-shaped vacuum" as some have suggested. The human spirit is either the residence of the Evil One or of the Triune God (I Jn. 3:10; Acts 26:18), and by faith-receptivity to the Person and work of Jesus Christ we become "partakers of the divine nature" (II Pet. 1:4), and "blessed with every spiritual blessing in the heavenly places" (Eph. 1:3). Jesus explained to His disciples, "If anyone loves Me, ...My Father will love him, and we (Father and Son and Spirit) will come to him, and make Our abode with Him" (Jn. 14:23). The Father,

Son, and Holy Spirit take up residence in the very core of our being, our spirit. To the Romans, Paul explained, "if the *Spirit* of Him who raised *Jesus* from the dead dwells in you, He (God the Father) who raised *Christ Jesus* from the dead will also give life to your mortal bodies through His *Spirit* who dwells in you" (Rom. 8:11). Note the three Persons of the Trinity.

The Father God dwells in us in order to have *koinonia* fellowship with us, and of necessity so does the Son, the living Lord Jesus, and the Spirit. The three divine Persons are one Being – the Triune God in us, allowing man to be man as God intended man to be. Jesus promised His disciples, "you will be in Me, and I in you" (Jn. 14:20). Paul reiterated the reality of the indwelling Jesus when he explained that the mystery of the gospel is "Christ in you, the hope of glory" (Col. 1:27), for "it is no longer I who lives, but Christ lives in me" (Gal. 2:20). "Christ is our life" (Col. 3:4), and that is the essential meaning of what it means to be a Christ-one, a Christian. It was a most illuminating question that Paul asked the Corinthian Christians, and one that many Christians today would be hard put to answer, "Do you not recognize that Jesus Christ lives in you? ...unless you believed in vain" (II Cor. 13:5). The primary awareness that one is a Christian is the recognition that Jesus Christ dwells within us and has become our life.

When the living Lord Jesus comes to live in the spirit of a receptive believer, in conjunction with the Father and the Spirit, He inhabits us, and the Christian is "in Christ," i.e. "in union with Christ." We "reign in life through the One, Jesus Christ" (Rom. 5:17). It should be noted that Jesus dwells in us as the eternal God-man – both His divinity and humanity come into play as He lives in us. He lived out humanness as the Perfect Man, and He desires to live it out perfectly in the humanity of each of us also. The purpose and goal is that "Christ be formed in us" (Gal. 4:19) in order to live out His character, i.e. by "the fruit of the Spirit" (Gal. 5:22,23).

"Those who are joined to the Lord, are one spirit with Him" (I Cor. 6:17), joined in spiritual union with the Triune God. Paul explained. "The Spirit bears witness with our spirit that we are children of God" – Christians (Rom. 8:16); and if "we do not have the Spirit of Christ, we are none of His" – not Christians (Rom. 8:9). To the Galatians, Paul notes a truth that is valid for all Christians, "God has sent forth the Spirit of His Son into our hearts" (Gal. 4:6). We have "the provision of the Spirit of Christ" (Phil. 1:19). The Spirit of God, the Spirit of Christ, within us is "the Spirit of life" (Rom. 8:2), the divine "Spirit who gives us life" (Jn. 6:63; II Cor. 3:6). Earlier we noted that "the last Adam became life-giving Spirit" (I Cor. 15:45), and Christians experience the vivifying internal presence of the Triune God.

Every genuine Christian has been given spiritual life again, regenerated by being "born of the Spirit" (John 3:1-6), "born again to a living hope through the resurrection of Jesus Christ from the dead" (I Peter 1:3), granted the divine life of the Triune God when we were "born of God" (Jn. 1:13; I Jn. 3:9; 5:1). We became "sons and daughters of God through faith in Christ Jesus" (Gal. 3:26), and "because we are sons, God has sent forth the Spirit of His Son into our hearts, crying 'Abba, Father'"(Gal. 4:6). The Christian individual is indwelt by the three Persons of the Trinity.

Christians have experienced a spiritual ontological exchange, whereby "the spirit that works in the sons of disobedience" (Eph. 2:2) has been replaced by the "Spirit of God who dwells in us" (Rom. 8:9), and He "wills and works for His good pleasure" (Phil. 2:13). We have been "turned from the dominion of Satan to God" (Acts 26:18), and "transferred from the domain of darkness into the kingdom of the beloved Son" (Col. 1:13). "If anyone is in Christ Jesus, they are a new creature; old spiritual things have passed away, and behold all has become new spiritually within them" (II Cor. 5:17). Christians are the "new creation" (Gal. 6:16) of God.

Christians participate personally and relationally with the tri-personal God, Father, Son, and Holy Spirit, who indwells every Christian, and He does so singularly (as One) but not separately; collectively but not individually. They are One in their divine, relational, Being as God, a singular indwelling of a plurality of three divine Persons, diversity in unity. That is difficult to maintain in our human thinking.

Perhaps you may be able to identify with the dilemma that I faced as a young junior high school (or middle school) young man (approximately seventh grade), when I went to youth group on Sunday evening.

I had never been inside of a church until I was approximately 11 years old, when my mother began to take the four children to church. So, having only heard the Christian vocabulary for about a year, I would listen to the leader of the youth group discussing an incident in the scriptures, and then he would ask a question about who was referred to in the text. My mind would be bouncing back and forth. "I know the answer is either God or Jesus, but I do not know which one is the right answer," and having a perfectionistic personality, I did not want to answer incorrectly and be subjected to embarrassment, so I would not answer. Let someone else take a stab at answering the question and risk being wrong! "Better to be silent and be thought an ignorant fool, than to open one's mouth and remove all doubt." I now know that there was no wrong answer in those options I was considering. God the Father and God the Son are singularly One and inseparable in their Being and function.

What we are attempting to illustrate in this diagram (*cf. Addendum M*) is to consider the implications of the Triune God indwelling us in such a manner that we are identified with the Father, Son and

Holy Spirit, and are invited and encouraged to participate in His divine Being and interactions. In Christian regeneration the Trinity comes to live in humanity, and humanity is brought into the Trinity. The Christian is "in Him," in His tri-personal Being, and He, the Triune God, is in us. What we call the "Christian life" is being alive in and with the Triune God to the extent that God and the individual human are interwoven spiritually in a "one spirit" union (cf. I Cor. 6:17); God and man interpenetrate one another; and we are meant to function perichoretically, i.e. in such a way that we move in the same space so seamlessly that it is not possible to tell whether it is He or me in action.

You will recall that when we were discussing how our Christian *theologia* must be based on the *oikonomia* of God's Self-revelation in Jesus Christ, we emphasized that the Being of God must not be constructed out of ideal and superlative mental constructs or substances, but it is imperative that Christians understand that the Being of God is relational. Now, at this point, as we discuss the *koinonia* of God's presence in Christians, we want to emphasize that our participation in the relational Being of God becomes the basis, the grace-provision, for all proper interpersonal relationships among human beings. The perfect personal relations of the Persons of the Triune God are intended to become the operative dynamic of all human interpersonal relationships.

That, I believe, is a primary reason why the Triune God created human beings. God did not create us because He was lonely sitting up there in the heavens all by Himself and needed some personal fellowship. Have you ever heard someone use that reasoning to explain God's action of creation? I have! It is absolutely ridiculous! First of all, it makes God's well-being contingent on the existence of humanity. For God to be the perfectly fulfilled relational God that He is requires us. Really? Is God dependent on man to be the God that He is? NO! We, on the other hand, are dependent on God to be man as God intended man to be. Second, such an explanation fails to take into account the Trinity. How could God be lonely if He eternally existed in the perfect relational interaction of three Persons in one relational Being? God is, within Himself, the essence of perfect relationality. That is why it is so meaningful when the apostle John twice writes, "God is LOVE" (I Jn. 4:8,16), knowing that love always flows out relationally to another, and divine love has done so between Father, Son and Holy Spirit from eternity. If God is not a Triune God, it would be necessary to remove the statement "God is LOVE" from our Bibles (cf. I Jn. 4:8,16), for love requires multiplicity and plurality of persons. Think about it! If there were not multiple personages in the Godhead wherein the love of the three could flow to one another prior to creating other creatures, angelic or human, then we would have to conclude that there was a time when God was not LOVE. Impossible! God is LOVE, always has been LOVE, and always will be relational LOVE.

The eternal unchangeable Triune God, in their eternal perfect interpersonal circle of LOVE, did what LOVE always does. They sought *others* to be participants in their circle of LOVE. LOVE always reaches out to *others*. Father, Son and Holy Spirit created human beings who were also personal beings, human beings, not divine beings, who could participate in personal love-relationship with the Triune God of the universe.

The point we need to emphasize is that when we think of the Trinity, this most important distinction of Christian thought, we should not think of numbers, of trying to fit three into one, or of a trisected three-part oneness. The Trinity is not to be conceptualized as mathematical or numerical. Instead of a numerical trinity, we must think of the relational Trinity, and the Persons of Father, Son and Holy Spirit in the perfect relationship of LOVE are the basis of all proper interpersonal relationships among human beings, in our marriages, our families, in our friendships, and in our churches. Our relationships in the Christian community must be derived from the relational LOVE of the Triune God.

There are some religious groups who call themselves "Christian" and emphasize family and social relationships, but deny the Trinity, the very basis of all proper relationships. In so doing, they cut the ground out from beneath their theological thinking and deny themselves of the very divine source of all true relationships. It doesn't make sense! Their's is a severed and disconnected theology.

The personal relationality of the Persons of the Trinity gives us the foundational grounding for all personal relations of man with God, and human beings with one another. So, the presence and function of the relational Trinity within the individual who receives God by faith becomes the operative basis of the collective Body of Christ, the Church. In Jesus' prayer to the Father in John 17, Jesus prayed, "that they may all be one; even as You, Father, *are* in Me and I in You, that they also may be in Us, ...The glory which You have given Me I have given to them, that they may be one, just as We are one; I in them and You in Me, that they may be perfected in unity..." (John 17:21-23). The inner relational function of the Trinity is to be the inner relational function of the Church, individuals filled with the Triune God collectively and corporately manifesting the character of God's relational LOVE. They will know we are Christians by our LOVE! That is why early observers of the church exclaimed, "See how they LOVE one another!" It was a unique relationality that stood out in the world around them. The lone-ranger attitude of solitary stand-alone self-sufficiency, as well as the self-centered quest for individualistic mysticism and an elitist access or intimacy with God, are incompatible with the relational Being and function of the Church, the collective Body of Christ. Paul wrote to the Corinthian Christians, "Even as the body is one, and yet has many members, and all the members of the body, though they are many, are one body, so also is Christ" (I Cor. 12:12). Just like the Trinity, the Church is comprised and functions via diversity in unity. Our Christian relationships in the Church and our ministry relationships to *others* in the world around us is to evidence that the Trinity is present with us (both individually and collectively) and functioning through us (cf. Rom. 12:4-8; I Cor. 12:4-6; Eph. 4:4-6).

As we mention the Church, we might note that the collective expression of the *koinonia* of the divine Trinity in the Church, would in the Greek language be the *ecclesia* expression of *koinonia* – another rhyming Greek word that could be utilized in our outline. *Theologia* ... *oikonomia* ... *koinonia* ... and we could subdivide the *koinonia* category into personal relational experience of the human individual with the Triune God, which in the Greek would be *empeiria*, and the collective relationship of the Church, the *ecclesia*.

Continuing our survey of how the *koinonia* participation and fellowship of the Christian and the Triune God affects every facet of our Christian lives, we consider the Christian's personal communion (*koinonia*), communication and conversation of prayer. This is an area where many Christians have struggled and have asked many questions. Prayer is the personal communication that every Christian is privileged to have in their personal relationship with the Triune God who has become their inner life. In His model prayer for His disciples, Jesus taught them to pray, "Our Father, who art in heaven, hallowed be Thy name..." (Matt. 6:9). Writing to the Corinthians, Paul refers to "all who in every place call upon the name of our Lord Jesus Christ" (I Cor. 1:2). Then, to the Roman Christians Paul mentions that "the Spirit helps our weakness; for we do not know how to pray as we should, but the Spirit Himself intercedes for us with groanings too deep for words" (Rom. 8:26). What we see here is that the indwelling presence of the Triune God is the divine facilitator of our prayers, even the pray-er prompting our prayers, whether uttered or inutterable, spoken or unspoken, to be shared heart to heart with the Father,

Son, and Holy Spirit. Christian prayer is part of this *koinonia* relationship that we have with the Triune God.

I recall an incident back in the mid 1970s, when I was presenting Quiet Time Conferences around the Midwest part of the United States. I was asked to come to a Christian college in Oklahoma City and share with the student body some ways that they could have a meaningful time alone with God each day. In the midst of the conference I was explaining how the Christian could commune and converse with the entire Triune God, Father, Son, and Holy Spirit. One of the risks one runs in speaking at such a religious educational institution is that the head of the theology department might disagree with you, and confront you about your theological orthodoxy (or heterodoxy, i.e. heresy). So he did, claiming that there was no biblical evidence suggesting that it was valid to pray to the Holy Spirit. I took him to the Romans 8:26,27 passage, but he did not find that convincing. The historical context in the mid 1970s was that the Charismatic Movement was burgeoning, spreading like wildfire, and traditional Evangelicalism was in a reactive mood that sought to diminish any emphasis on the Holy Spirit. I look back on that incident and believe, just as I did then, that the theological professor had an inadequate and deficient understanding of the Trinity, and no discernable understanding of the Triune *koinonia* that we are discussing.

In like manner, all of Christian worship, both individual and corporate, should be prompted by the presence of the Triune God within us. Listen to the words of Paul in Eph. 3:14-19 and note the reference to all three Persons of the Trinity and how this should lead us to worship.

> "For this reason I bow my knees before the **Father**, from whom every family in heaven and on earth derives its name, that He would grant you, according to the riches of His glory, to be strengthened with power through His **Spirit** in the inner man, so that **Christ** may dwell in your hearts through faith; *and* that you, being rooted and grounded in love, may be able to comprehend with all the saints what is the breadth and length and height and depth, and to know the love of **Christ** which surpasses knowledge, that you may be filled up to all the fullness of **God**."

Earlier in his letter to the Ephesians, Paul explained, "through Him (Jesus Christ) we both (Jew and Gentile, irrespective of nationality and ethnicity) have our access in one Spirit to the Father" (Eph. 2:18).

An interesting exercise is to go through the New Testament and note how often the doxological statements, the worship statements of the writers of the new covenant documents, make reference to all three Persons of the Triune God. One example: "The grace of the Lord Jesus Christ, and the love of God (the Father), and the fellowship (*koinonia*) of the Holy Spirit, be with you all" (II Cor. 13:14). I am confident that you have heard the pastor use that as a benedictory doxology in church services.

The very purpose for which God created us as human beings is fulfilled and brought to fruition as the Triune God dwells in and functions through Christian individuals and the Church. Isaiah 43:7 indicates that we were "created for His glory," and Isaiah also declares that "God does not give His glory to another" (Isa. 42:8; 48:11). Only God, the Triune God, can manifest His all-glorious character of godliness within His creation (and specifically in the behavior of created human beings) in such a manner that brings glory to Himself. God's glorification is brought about by the indwelling of the Trinity in Christian individuals and in the corporate Church, the Body of Christ, so that "with one accord we may with one voice glorify the God and Father of our Lord Jesus Christ" (Rom. 15:6) and "do all to the glory of God" (I Cor. 10:31).

It should be evident that *koinonia* is what the relational Triune God desires to facilitate with humanity, and has acted in history through the Son by the power of the Holy Spirit (*oikonomia*) to effect such a genuine personal relationship between the divine Being of God and a human being who is receptive to such relationship in faith. That is the "good news" of the gospel, the intimate connection of a personal relation between God and man that permeates to the level of spiritual union. This is what allows man to be man as God intended man to be, in the fulfillment of the fact that we were "created for His glory." God in us, and we in God.

The relational *koinonia* of the Christian and the Triune God allows the individual Christian and the Church of Jesus Christ to delight in the Trinitarian Deity of Father, Son and Spirit. We experience "glimpses of glory" wherein we learn to appreciate divine beauty, and love, and joy, and the real pleasures of life that He created for us.

But we must note that this *koinonia* with the Triune God is not always a euphoric joy. The apostle Paul writes of his desire to participate in the "fellowship (*koinonia*) of His (Christ's) sufferings" (Phil. 3:10). Participating in the *pathos* of Jesus' sufferings involves the opposition, tribulation and hatred of this fallen world, energized as it is by the diabolic "ruler of this world" (Jn. 12:31; 14:30; 16:11), who as the "tempter" sets his evil sights on the destruction of those who are identified with Christ as "Christians." Satan hates "Christ in us" as much as he hated the Christ who lived on earth two millennia ago, and will continue to do everything in his limited power to discourage our *koinonia* and cause us to misrepresent the character of Christ in our behavior.

Correlation of the Categories

It is now time to correlate and compare the three categories of *theologia, oikonomia,* and *koinonia* in order to see how they relate and connect with one another, comprising the fullness of the gospel. We can see their respective emphases by first placing the three categories in parallel columns. (cf. *Addendum N*)

Theologia pertains to the consideration of the essence of who God is in Himself, whereas *oikonomia* considers God at work in human history, and *koinonia* looks at God at work in us. We have the Triune God as formulated in Christian thinking, the Triune God historically revealed in the Son, and the Triune God in Christian experience. Theological speculation; historical manifestation; and personal appreciation of the Triune God. *Theologia* is often human speculation about God; *oikonomia* addresses the revelation of God; and *koinonia* pertains to our participation in God. Human consideration of God; the redemptive work of God in Christ; and the personal fellowship of mankind with God.

Theologia often becomes a form of philosophical theology, whereas *oikonomia* is the explanation of the redemptive theology of God via the Son, Jesus Christ, and *koinonia* is the spiritual theology (or restorative theology) of the Triune God once again operative in human individuals, joined spiritually with a human being to allow "man to be man as God intended man to be."

Some have referred to the consideration of the Triune God in *theologia* as the study of the Immanent Trinity, or ontological Trinity or essential Trinity, looking at God to ponder His essential Being within Himself, the relational and internal interaction of the Triune God *a se* (in Himself). *Oikonomia*, on the other hand, is viewing the Triune God as the Economic Trinity, the operational Trinity, or the administrative Trinity, how God worked or operated to implement His redemptive plan in the Son, the Self-communication of the Triune God *per adventum*, i.e. in the appearance and advent of Jesus Christ. The *koinonia* category (and it must be admitted that this category has not been part of traditional and historical Christian theological conversation, but I have added this personal and experiential category because it has been tragically neglected throughout so much of Christian thinking. There is a need to consider what I am calling the "conjunctive Trinity," or the perichoretic Trinity, with an emphasis on our human spiritual union with the Trinity. Human beings can be conjoined spiritually with the Triune God in a "one spirit" union (cf. I Cor. 6:17), to the extent that God and the human individual, as well as the collective Body of Christ, are seen to "move around in the same place/space," which is the meaning of the Greek word *perichoresis. Koinonia* considers the relational Self-communication of the Triune God *ad diversum*, i.e. toward and involving others. The perfect loving relations of Father, Son, and Holy Spirit (*theologia*) could not be kept to themselves. LOVE always seeks to involve others, i.e. US!

When mankind attempts to understand God using only his human finite understanding and wisdom, he inevitably has a very limited perspective of God. He has an *apophatic* theology, meaning that it is "apart from the speech," the revelation of God by means of the Word of God, Jesus Christ. *Apophatic* theology is also called *anaphatic* theology, meaning "without speech," often emphasizing that God is so "wholly other" than man that he is incapable of human explication. In the category of *oikonomia* we recognize that the Triune God has revealed Himself historically in time, and subsequently we can have *kataphatic* theology, meaning "according to speech" in the manner that God has revealed Himself in the Word, Jesus Christ. Once again, I have coined a new phrase that adds to the two labels that have been used for centuries in Christian thought – I have introduced the phrase *eisophatic* theology, meaning that on a personal, relational level, God "speaks into" our hearts via a personal revelation that is "caught, not taught." Therein we have a very personal, experiential theology.

There is a sense in which there is always a sense of *apophatic* theology in our human understanding of God, for our finite minds can never comprehend the infinite essence of who God IS in the depths of His internal relational Being. There is always a sense of "mystery" in our knowing of God! God did, however, intend to make Himself known to mankind, for we can really only know Him to the extent that He has chosen to make Himself known, and the Triune God has done just that in the historic knowability of God via the Revelation of God the Son, Jesus Christ. But the purpose and objective of the historic and redemptive revelation of the Son was not just a history lesson or a theological corpus of doctrinal information. It was that we might have the opportunity to experience an intimate personal knowing of God by means of personal revelation, allowing the internal spiritual indwelling of the Father, Son, and Spirit to become our LIFE in personal relationship, wherein they become the dynamic of the behavioral expression of His character in our daily lives.

Using many of the same words and phrases used in the foregoing comparative columns, we proceed to use a more diagrammatic illustration (cf. *Addendum O*), using the figures that we used when considering the three categories previously. We do so in order to see how the categories of *theologia*, *oikonomia*, and *koinonia* transition and flow from one to the other, in order to constitute the whole of the gospel.

There is no need to go through the terms we have just discussed again, but we should note that some additional words are employed on this diagram. At the top and bottom of the diagram there are the words "OBJECTIVE" and "SUBJECTIVE" respectively. "Objective" refers to that which is external and outside of us. The Triune God, in the immensity of the infinity of His omnipresence is incapable of being fully contained in me, or you, or even the world as we know it. So, *theologia* is represented as outside of us on the diagram. Likewise, the entire history of the redemptive mission of the physical life and work of Jesus Christ is outside of us in the "objective" realm. But the activity of God in the objective and historic life and work of Jesus Christ (*oikonomia*) culminates in the resurrection, ascension, and Pentecostal outpouring of the Spirit of Christ whereby the person and work of the living Lord Jesus can be appropriated within receptive individuals, and that is where we note the connection that flows down into the realm of the "subjective," that which transpires internally within the human individual who is the "subject" in this case. The objective and rather abstract understanding of the Triune God (*theologia*) is tangibilized in the advent and redemptive mission of Jesus Christ (*oikonomia*), and then is personalized in the relationship that receptive human individuals have with the indwelling presence of the Triune God (*koinonia*).

This diagram also attempts to demonstrate the links between the categories by employing two additional Greek words, *kenosis* and *theosis*. The process by which God began to act and to intersect with human history in the Self-revelation of Himself involved the Self-emptying of the Son of God in order to come to earth and function as a human being. This reality is recorded in Philippians 2:5-7: "Christ Jesus, although He existed in the form of God, did not regard equality with God a thing to be held on to, but *emptied* Himself, taking the form of a bondservant, and being made in the likeness of men..." In the phrase indicating that the Son "*emptied* Himself," the Greek root word is *kenosis*. The Son of God emptied Himself of the prerogatives of direct divine activity, in order to function within the hypostatic union of divine-human being, doing nothing of His own initiative (Jn. 5:19,30; 8:28; 12:49), but allowing "the Father abiding in Him to do His works" (Jn. 14:10). So the transition from *theologia* to *oikonomia* was effected in the kenotic Self-emptying of the Son of God to function as a human being indwelt and energized by the Father for every moment in time for 33 years. Never less than God; never more than man, "the Word became flesh" (Jn. 1:14) in the incarnation.

The movement that connects the category of *oikonomia* to *koinonia* is identified with the Greek word *theosis*, a word that we have referred to previously. Though not used in the inspired scriptures (as is *kenosis*), this word was used in the early thinking of the Greek-speaking church, and referred to the process by which the Triune God is relationally in-godded within receptive and faithful human individuals, and thus collectively in the Body of Christ, the Church. The very divine character and dynamic energies of Triune God-ness come to indwell and function in Christians, even though humans who have become Christians do not become God essentially in some form of deification or divinization, or in some form of monistic pantheism. *Theosis* is the word that the Eastern Orthodox Christian Churches legitimately use, and have used for almost two millennia, to explain the process of God's work of salvation and sanctification within Christians.

Note the connection of the outpouring of the Spirit on Pentecost (*oikonomia*) to the spiritual indwelling and infilling of the Triune God in the Christian (*koinonia*), from an objective historical event on Pentecost, to the subjective presence of the Triune God within all believers.

It is interesting to observe that in the transition from *theologia* to *oikonomia*, "the Word *became* flesh" (Jn. 1:14), the Physical Christ. In the transition from *oikonomia* to *koinonia,* we previously noted that "the second Adam *became* life-giving Spirit" (I Cor. 15:45), the Pneumatic Christ. In both transitions we observe Christ becoming, and taking on, a new form. There was no change in His essential divine Being as the Son of God, but in each case there is a "becoming" whereby the Son takes on a differing form of expression. The Word became flesh, the Physical Christ, by means of the hypostatic union of Deity and humanity in the one Person of Jesus Christ. Christ. The last Adam became the life-giving Spirit, the Pneumatic Christ, who in Spirit-form enters into "spirit-union" (cf. I Cor. 6:17) with human individuals. Why do we seldom hear this pointed out in Christian teaching? Traditional Christian thought does not want to go there!

We shall proceed, then, to point out why there has been such an aversion in the history of the Church to accepting, teaching and proclaiming the glorious reality of the *koinonia* participation of Christians with the Triune God. The entire category of *koinonia* has been treated somewhat as a suspicious step-child in the preaching of the gospel (*kerygma*). Christian theology has not even applied a generally accepted label to this theological category. It has simply been a sub-point of *oikonomia*, generally regarded as the personal application of how human individuals might respond to the history and theology of the Christian message. It is hard to find any theological discourse among Western theological thinkers that expands the discussion into what we are calling "*koinonia*." Western theology has found it convenient to slide the subjective implications of the revealed gospel of the living Lord Jesus "under the rug," neglecting the experiential realities of Christian life or denying them altogether, usually relegating such "personal" matters to a hazy and ambiguous psychologized "feel-good religion" with the promise of fantastic idealized benefits reserved for the future.

Theologia and *oikonomia* have been part of Christian theological conversation from the earliest centuries. The Greek-speaking Eastern Orthodox Christian Churches have always used these terms, and do so to this day. Roman Catholic theology uses these terms, as noted in the 1994 edition of *The Catechism of the Catholic Church*, pg. 236:

> "The Fathers of the Church distinguish between theology (*theologia*) and economy (*oikonomia*). "Theology" refers to the mystery of God's inmost life within the Blessed Trinity and "economy" to all the works by which God reveals himself and communicates his life. Through the *oikonomia* the *theologia* is revealed to us; but conversely, the *theologia* illuminates the whole *oikonomia*. God's works reveal who he is in himself; the mystery of his inmost being enlightens our understanding of all his works."

Although American Evangelical thinkers seldom concern themselves with these categories, the mainline Protestant theologians such as T.F. Torrance, Wolfhart Pannenberg, Jürgen Moltmann, Christoph Schwoebel, Robert W. Jenson, etc. definitely address these categories. Karl Rahner, the German Catholic theologian formulated what is known as "Rahner's Rule" concerning the Trinity by stating, "*Theologia* is *oikonomia*, and *oikonomia* is *theologia*." Though I would disagree with his statement as it stands, I would concur that *theologia* must be informed by *oikonomia*, and *oikonomia* must be informed by *theologia*, for they are mutually interdependent, demanding reciprocal input for the development of objective theological discussion.

Western theological discussion (both Catholic and Protestant) has, for the most part, remained in the objective categories of *theologia* and *oikonomia*, unwilling to venture into the realm of the subjective participation of God with man and man with God, that the Eastern Church identifies as "*theosis*." The Western Church shies away from any mention of the Self-investiture of the Triune God to unite and participate with an individual human believer and the collective Church. Apart from some discussions of "spirituality," employing various spiritual disciplines, exercises, and mentors, the Western Church has followed the path of over-objectification, and avoidance of meaningful explanation of internal experiential implications of the spiritual union of the Triune God with mankind.

Why has the Western Church followed this course of action? Not only has there been a suspicious aversion to the *theosis* teaching of the Eastern Church, but much of the Western Church (both Roman Catholic and Protestant) constructed their theological system on anthropological presuppositions that disavowed and disallowed consideration of the subjective and experiential function of human individuals. Augustine (A.D. 354-430) laid the foundation for such teaching with his explanation that the fall of Adam into sin rendered all humanity guilty for sin, and as a consequence the abilities of human function were intrinsically altered causing man's internal psychological faculties to be inherently and innately defective and dysfunctional, being debased, depraved, despoiled and deviant. The *essentia humanum* of fallen humanity was regarded as essentially evil, and ontologically vitiated and reduced to a sub-human level. The inner being of mankind was deemed to be incapable of responding to the actions of God in Jesus Christ by an intrinsic "bondage of the will" that disallowed any genuine relational interaction with the Triune God. The redemptive *oikonomia* of the life and work of Jesus Christ could only be applied to human persons by the prior divine determinism that arbitrarily selected certain persons as the "elect." When the alleged "elect" were divinely imputed with the benefits of Christ's work in a completely objectified and positional manner, this did not affect or alter the individual's incapacitated subjective and experiential function, leaving the Christian as but a "saved sinner" incapable of any genuine *koinonia* with the Triune God, never to be restored to be man as God intended man to be in personal relationship with the Father, Son, and Holy Spirit, except perhaps in a future realm and time.

This Augustinian-Calvinist perspective of the condition of fallen humanity, which pervades such a large percentage of Christian understanding to this very day, preempts any real personal understanding and participation in the *koinonia* that we have documented from the new covenant scriptures.

A more recent theological formulation in Western Protestantism, self-designated as "Evangelical Calvinism" or "Trinitarianism," has become prominent in the late 20th century and early 21st century. It retains the anthropological assumptions of Augustine that have prevailed since the 4th century, and therefore is also unable to give any credence to the truly relational subjective experience of *koinonia* in a spiritual union of God and human individuals. Though they have jettisoned the thesis of "limited atonement" reserved for special "elect" individuals, this novel adaptation of Calvinism indicates that Jesus Christ is the "Elect One" in whom ALL humanity participates in the vicarious experience of His *oikonomia*. Jesus was the substitutional replacement for all human individuals, having experienced every event of His life on earth "as us," and thereby effected an ontological exchange of all human being from an inherent condition of subhuman corruption to a universal assumption of applied redeemed-being. This transference of all humanity into the historic *oikonomia* experience of Jesus vicariously, does not lead to a truly subjective and relational *koinonia* experience of an individual with the Triune God, but leaves the Christian with an objectified logical identification with the historic experience of Jesus – a mind-game!

Continuing to consider why the Western Church seems to be averse to accepting and experiencing the *koinonia* participation of the Triune God with Christian people, we must (to be fair) note some attempts within the Western Church to venture toward this subjective and experiential fellowship with God. In the history of the Roman Catholic Church there are a number of designated "saints" and "mystics" who referred to "mystical union" with God and wrote of deep personal intimacy in their subjective experience of fellowship with God. They have often been regarded as a special spiritual elite to be adored and emulated, with the recognition that most normal Christians will not have the time, inclination, or "calling" to achieve such closeness with God. They are still widely read among Christian peoples of all theological persuasions. The Roman Catholics (and a few Protestant groups) have long espoused various procedures to achieve some level of "spirituality" via spiritual disciplines and regular participation in the "real presence of Jesus" via the Eucharistic practice of the Church.

In the history of Western Protestantism there are also some movements that have attempted to address experiential fellowship with God. Some of the Anabaptist groups and the German Pietist movement come to mind. The Moravians had an influence upon John Wesley, and within his Arminian orientation to theology he advocated small groups with practical methods (thus Methodism) whereby they would encourage one another to personal holiness and social involvement, but these often bogged down in legalistic proceduralism. The Pentecostal movement that began in the early 20th century and morphed into the Charismatic movement of the mid-20th century was an attempt to break out of the sterile ecclesiasticism of the mainline churches and experience the Spirit of God, but they often became so enamored by their spiritual power-gifts they lost sight of the character implications of the gospel that bring glory to God. There have been quite a number of other Protestant movements that have emphasized the inner spiritual life of the Christian individual. The Keswick movement in England spawned emphases on a "deeper life," a "higher life," "an abundant life," "a victorious life," an "exchanged life," and eventually to a "union life" wherein a Christian could focus on his or her spiritual identity in order to be convinced of "who they were in Christ." All of these emphases fell short of advocating the full experience of *koinonia* fellowship and participation with the Triune

God that is the privilege of every Christian in the new covenant community.

The "union life" movement did have some emphasis on the advocacy of the *koinonia* union and participation with and in the Triune God that we have attempted to illustrate in this study, but portions of that movement failed to recognize that the Christian's spiritual union with God is a relational union, and not an essential union. The Christian does not become God, neither Father, Son, or Holy Spirit. The distinction between Christ and the Christian must always be maintained. The living Christ does not replace our humanity, destroy our individuality or personality, or cause a transmorphing of the human into God. The assertion of "Christ as us," popular in the "Union Life Movement, can (and did) slide into a form of monistic pantheism (despite their redefinition of pan*en*theism). The "union life" movement was thus marginalized, and by their abuses and overstatements served only to make the mainline Western Protestant churches even more suspicious and cautious of any who might emphasize the inner subjective life of spiritual union with the Triune God.

From the early decades of the 16th century Protestant Reformation there has been a predisposition against allowing Christian thought to move into the subjective category of *koinonia*. An early Lutheran reformer, Andreas Osiander (1498-1552), rejected the idea that justification was only an objective, legal and forensic declaration and imputation of Christ's "alien righteousness," as was the teaching of Luther under the influence of Melanchthon. Osiander argued that divine righteousness comes from God in Christ dwelling in the Christian by faith, that Christians can actually participate (*koinonia*) in Christ and His righteousness. Both John Calvin and the Lutheran Formula of Concord (1557) rejected the idea that the indwelling of Christ had any connection to Christian justification and righteousness, and Protestants, in general, have ever since been suspicious of the teaching of the indwelling of the Triune God. They always seek to keep Christian thought objectified in *theologia* and *oikonomia*, and the juridical implications of such.

Contemporary American Evangelicalism continues to avoid the intra-personal relationality of the Triune God with human beings in *koinonia*, the very purpose for which we were created. They offer instead the reheated smorgasbord of their respective ecclesiastical agendas, encouraging God's people to get more involved in churchy busyness, to be more committed and dedicated and consecrated to "the cause" *de jour*. They admonish the people in the pew to engage in human self-effort to read their bibles more often, pray more often, tithe ten percent, attend church services regularly, serve on committees, (and almost as a footnote) to serve the social needs of others. They contend that these "works" activities will draw people closer to fellowship with God and with one another in a productive religious community. How tragic that modern evangelicalism is so ignorant of the genuine grace-invigorated new covenant community and the *koinonia* of the living *ecclesia*.

So now, if you were wondering why what you are reading in this book is not what you hear in your local churches, I have attempted to provide you with some perspective of the aversion that most leaders in the institutional church today have toward the clear biblical pattern of the Triune God's intent to invest Himself (Father, Son, and Holy Spirit) in genuine internal and indwelling relational participation with Christian persons, with you and me, and us together in Him! When Christian individuals attempt to share the "good news" of the indwelling life and love of Jesus, and spiritual union with the Triune God, they are often met with suspicion or outright repudiation by church leaders, for this message does not appear to advance the success of their programs. Everything in popular religion seems to look askance at such subjective and experiential explanations of *koinonia*.

Oh, yes, there are some voices crying in the wilderness, but the institutional Church, as a whole, is not interested. They have a bias against such subjective concerns of what goes on spiritually inside of the Christian believer. They adamantly retain their teaching on the historical *oikonomia* and doctrinal *theologia*. Meanwhile God continues to speak to the hearts of individuals, wherever they might be, who yearn for intimacy with His Triune Being, and He reveals to them via personal revelation that is caught not taught what He desires to be and do in them. It is personal, and relational, and intimate fellowship with the three

Persons of the Triune God, and therein with one another in the Church!

Some might wonder whether the emphasis on the Triune God being made in this study diminishes or overshadow the Christocentric emphasis that some of us have emphasized. NEVER! Perhaps the diagram of the Christocentric Emphasis of God's Revelation (*cf. Addendum P*) will provide some perspective.

Our Christian thinking must always retain a Christocentric perspective and focal point. The proper and legitimate starting point and approach to Christian thought is to orient all of our thinking to the historical Person and work of Jesus Christ, expressed in the category of *oikonomia*. Our *theologia* must be informed by, developed on the basis of, and derived from the Christological and soteriological narrative of *oikonomia*. Our knowledge of God is limited to the revelation of Jesus Christ alone, for Jesus told Philip, "If you had known Me, you should have known My Father also ... He that has seen Me, has seen the Father" (Jn. 14:7,9). The Triune God is revealed by the Son of God. Jesus Christ is the Revelator, the *prima facie* (primary face) historic visibility of the invisible God.

Likewise, the intimate relationality of experiential Christian *koinonia* with the Triune God and others must also be informed by, and derived from the historic Christological and soteriological narrative of *oikonomia*. The center-point of the gospel record and Christian thought must always be Jesus Christ, the Son of God who revealed the Father and pointed to the full and complete sufficiency of Himself as the vital ontological means of allowing humanity to participate in intimate personal relationality with the Triune God.

But there has been a repetitive tendency in Western Christian thought to focus on the historic Person and work of Jesus Christ (*oikonomia*), particularly noting Jesus' exclamation from the cross, "It is finished!" (John 19:30). No doubt the *oikonomia* is complete, and explains the historic focal point of the "Finished Work" of Jesus Christ. However, various interpretations of the "finished work" of Jesus have led to a perspective of the terminal finality of Jesus' work and Christian thought at the time of, and in the events of, Jesus' death and resurrection. This is a tragic short-circuiting of the Triune God's intent to draw all human beings into personal participation of Himself in "abundant life" (Jn. 10:10) in every ensuing age. The *oikonomia* is not limited to the redemptive "fixing of the sin problem;" it is the ever-expanding center point of God's intent to draw all mankind into participation in the loving relational reality of His Triune life in *koinonia*.

My friend and correspondent, Mr. David Avilla, expressed this tendency of Western theological thinking in this manner: "A large portion of the church has focused on redemption with a narrow focus on objective justification. When that concern is addressed through believing in a proper or acceptable 'theory of atonement,' then there is a strong tendency to experientially park on the side of the spiritual road with our hoods up, waiting for the heavenly AAA to come by and pick us up to take us to our heavenly destination." I think that is a poignant, sharply perceptive picture of how traditional Christian thought has sidelined the continuing and ongoing work of God in Christ and by the Spirit (*koinonia*), and focused on the teleological end-destiny of human individuals.

Historic evangelical thought has treated the work of the cross and the subsequent event of the resurrection of Jesus as the terminus of Christian thought, pointing out with logical sterility that "death could not hold Him" (cf. Acts 2:24). The redemptive cross-work is viewed as the terminal "stop sign" of Christian thought, the "full stop" as the British say, the conclusive "period" and end to God's action in Jesus Christ, as if the work of God, the activity of God, God's revealing of Himself was terminated and concluded at the crucifixion of Jesus on the cross (and subsequent resurrection). God is eternally the God who reveals Himself. He knows full well the need of His creation for such revelation of Himself through His Son and by His Spirit. Particularly, for the continuing revealing work of the Pneumatic Christ (cf. I Cor. 15:45) who woos mankind into ever-deeper *koinonia* and sharing in the relational dynamic of the Triune God.

Conversely, those who stress a Christ-centered Christian theology, and emphasize the indwelling life of the risen and living Lord Jesus might be (and have been) criticized for an overemphasis on the second Person of the Godhead, and charged with failing to maintain a more complete and unified teaching of the Triune Godhead. This is usually an undue and misguided criticism of Christic emphasis, for it is always Jesus the Son who is the revelatory personage of the Godhead, and the continuing pneumatic manifestation of the Godhead in the lives of God's receptive people.

No doubt, it is possible to develop a form of Christomonism whereby Christ is elevated to a supremacy that diminishes or subdues the Father and the Spirit, as evidenced by the fact that Karl Barth has been charged with Christomonism by some of his theological critics. The new covenant biblical witness certainly points to the necessity of "preaching Christ" (Acts 5:42; Rom. 15:19,20), and Him crucified (I Cor. 2:2), as the revelator of God, the Lord and Savior of mankind, and the continuing manifestation of God in the form of the Holy Spirit. So let us never forget the centrality of Jesus Christ, and remember the word of Paul to Timothy that Jesus is the "one mediator between God and men"(I Tim. 2:5).

It is important to note and illustrate (*cf.* *Addendum Q*) that the complete process of moving from *theologia* to *oikonomia* to *koinonia* is not only to demonstrate how the relational Trinity of God (*theologia*), displayed in the advent of the Son and His Self-sacrificial death (*oikonomia*), allows the three Persons of the Trinity – Father, Son, and Holy Spirit – to indwell and reside in human individuals (*koinonia*), but to show the equally important reality that persons who are receptive to such relationship with God are also "in the Trinity," drawn into the perfect circle of the Triune LOVE. That was the desire of divine LOVE, to include "others", because LOVE always reaches out to "others," into their loving relational interactions. That is why the Triune divine Being created angelic and human beings to incorporate them into the loving community (common-unity) of Trinitarian LOVE.

Utilizing the same triple-line concentric circle that was used originally to illustrate the perfect circle of LOVE between Father, Son, and Holy Spirit, it is now expanded to include every person who is receptive to participating in Trinitarian *koinonia*. It has often been noted that there are far more biblical statements about our being "in Christ," than there are references to "Christ in us," and likewise to being "in the Spirit," than to the Spirit being in us, evidencing that our inclusion in the Trinity is equally important as the residence of the Trinity in us. The focus must be on the Triune God, and not on us! Another way of illustrating the reality of humanity participating within the loving interrelations of the Trinity can be viewed (cf. *Addendum R*), showing Christian individuals within the triple concentric circles representing the interrelations of divine love.

All humanity is invited to participate in the perfect *koinonia* relations of the Trinity. The wide-open arms of Father, Son, and Holy Spirit desire to enfold every person in the eternal circle of divine LOVE. The opportunity is extended to every human individual to experience the joyous beauty and peace of God's ever-inclusive LOVE, and the satisfaction and fulfillment of functioning relationally as God intended man to function. But there is not an automatic inclusion of all humanity into the perichoretic dance of *koinonia*, as some have suggested (and I am thinking particularly of those who allege a vicarious replacement of all humanity into the *oikonomia* of Christ's life, function and experience, labeled as "Trinitarianism" aka "Evangelical Calvinism").

The inspired scriptures of the new covenant literature have an abundance of reference to the opportunity for the individual human being to respond to God's Self-revelation in Christ by the receptivity of faith. God created humanity as choosing creatures whose choices have consequences, and God respects the freedom of choice with which He created us. He does not coerce us into fellowship with Himself via a process of divine determinism. That would be a mechanical and positional identification, rather than a freely chosen personal relationship and *koinonia* with the relational Persons (*theologia*) of the Triune Godhead. Via the choice of human receptivity of the divine activity of the Triune God, any (and all) human individuals can avail themselves of participation with, and in God by faith.

None are "railroaded" or coerced into this beautiful *koinonia* fellowship with God. God does not "sweep" every human person into this circle of LOVE by means of an inclusive universalism. God respects our freedom of choice to the extent that we can reject His tri-personal LOVE. A human individual can say, "No thanks, God. I am not interested," or even, "Take your love, and shove it!" For most of us that seems like an inconceivable possibility, but God loves us that much, to allow a person to reject His Triune relational love, and to fail to fulfill the very purpose of human existence.

It needs to be said before we continue to the conclusion: The indwelling of the personal Triune God that allows for Christian *koinonia* is an already personal, spiritual reality for every genuine Christian. The presence of the Father, Son, and Holy Spirit in the Christian is not something we need to seek to acquire or achieve, as the Eastern Orthodox Churches have often propounded in their teaching on *theosis*. The only question we need ask ourselves as Christians is, "Are we enjoying the fellowship, the *koinonia*, the participation in our relational union with the Triune God? The grace-dynamic implicit in *koinonia* can free us from all the performance requirements of religion. Joy inexpressible is ours to appreciate as we derive the character of God in our behavior unto the glory of God.

Conclusion

We began this study by noting that early Christian thinkers followed the methodology of Greek philosophy, speculating about a god-box full of superlatives, and projecting an insuperable, dualistic distance between God and man, creating a transcendent and inaccessible God that prevented any real connection with created mankind. Distinctive Christian thought, on the other hand, must take into account the communicability between the relational Being of the Triune God and mankind. The Son of God was incarnated as the God-man for the purpose of uniting God with human beings, but not elevating human beings to God-ness. By the kenotic Self-emptying of the Son of God, and the humiliation of His death on the cross, and His resurrection, ascension and Pentecostal outpouring, God makes Himself available for genuine connection and relational *koinonia* union with human beings who are receptive to such.

When the Church fails to understand and proclaim the relational Trinity, historically demonstrated in the redemption narrative recorded in the new covenant literature, and issuing forth in a genuine experiential participation of Christians with the Triune God, then the Christian message veers into Deism, with a detached, merely conceptual idea of a pseudo-Trinity that is "out there" at a distance and inaccessible for real personal communion. Worse yet, it becomes a form of idolatry, which is the construction and worship of an object that is not God, or not worthy of God. An idol may be a material object made of wood or stone, or it may be an immaterial object such as a mental concept, or emotional memory, or a conceptual ideal that is inadequate and misrepresents the relational Triune God of Father, Son, and Holy Spirit. God does not take idolatry lightly!

Of late, in the latter part of the 20th and first part of the 21st centuries, the Church at large has been giving more attention to the revelation of God in Jesus Christ and by the Holy Spirit, articulating the relational Being of the Triune God. It is a tragedy, though, that Christian thinkers do not want to go beyond the historic presentation (*oikonomia*) and the doctrinal formulation (*theologia*) of Christ. They do not want to consider the *koinonia* of actual participation of individual human beings in the loving interactions of the Triune God. When they do this they short-circuit the intent of the gospel, and turn the *oikonomia* of God's Self-revelation into but an interesting vignette of human history on which theologians have constructed the static explanation of Christian religion, a mockery of the genuine relationship between God and man.

Protestant Christians have often been faulted for an inordinate emphasis on the importance and authority of scripture, for accessing and learning the details of the Bible as an end in itself (Bible trivia), for implying that salvation is "knowing the Bible," or even displaying church signs that declare, "The Bible Saves!" They should know better than to engage in such misrepresentation.

It is important to explain the necessity of a *relational* approach to the inspired scriptures, rather than merely a mental, informational approach to Bible knowledge. It has been said, "The Bible is the only book in the world where one must *know the Author* personally, relationally, and experientially in order to understand the Book." If *koinonia* participation with the Trinity is not an intimate reality in a Christian's life, they are inevitably struggling in the reading and understanding of the scriptures!

Likewise, the Christian understanding of the relational Triune God is the only concept of God ever presented to humanity that requires an individual be drawn into the experience of the relational Trinity of LOVE in order to understand and appreciate God as He really is, as Father, Son, and Holy Spirit in love relation with one another, the import of the life and work of Jesus Christ, and the *koinonia* participation that God desires with receptive Christians. So, if God seems far away in your Christian experience, then perhaps the teaching you have received in your church has "sold you short" and given you "the short end of the stick," failing to adequately introduce you to the *koinonia* with God that can and will revitalize your Christian under-standing and your delight in the new covenant scriptures. Our *koinonia* experience with the Triune God must and will inform and enlighten our *theologia* understanding, drawing us ever closer and deeper into the intimacy of the circle of love of the personal interactions of the divine Trinity.

On a personal level, "The Triune God in Christian Thought and Experience" has had a great impact on my thinking and worship. I am convinced that I will never be able to think of the trajectory of the Christian gospel henceforth without seeing it's point of commencement in the relational Triune God, and it's intended consummation in personal union and fellowship (*koinonia*) with the Triune God. This personal relationality with the Triune God is the "key" to seeing and appreciating the fullness of the Christian gospel.

It is imperative that Christians understand that the objective of Christian *theologia* and *oikonomia* is to experience Christian *koinonia*, fellowship with God and with His Son Jesus in the Spirit, and with one another in Christian unity in the Church of Jesus Christ. There is such a need for Christians to be subjectively, intimately involved in participation with the Triune God, to experience the fullness of the interiority of Father, Son and Holy Spirit, to the extent of recognizing our interpenetration with God. God's loving heart desires that we, His creatures, might share in the relational circle of His Triune Love and function, experientially, intimately, emotionally, the Triune God in us, and we in Him.

The Christian faith is the entirety and fullness of the tri-personal Being of God (Father, Son, and Holy Spirit), operative in the entirety of the tri-functional human being (spirit and soul and body – cf. I Thess. 5:23), drawing said human beings into ever-deeper participation in the divine life and fellowship of the Triune God, and the expression of that living divine-human fellowship in the relationships of the Body of Christ, the community of the Triune God, the Church. The whole of the gospel, the whole of the Christian faith, the whole of salvation, the whole of the Church of Jesus Christ is predicated on our awareness of and participation in the inseparable personal relationality of the Triune God.

The words of the Apostle Paul to the Ephesian Christians seem to be a most fitting conclusion to this study of "the Triune God in Christian Thought and experience:"

Ephesians 3:14-19 – "[14] For this reason I bow my knees before the *Father*, [15] from whom every family in heaven and on earth derives its name, [16] that He would grant you, according to the riches of His glory, to be strengthened with power through His *Spirit* in the inner man, [17] so that *Christ* may dwell in your hearts through faith; and that you, being rooted and grounded in love, [18] may be able to comprehend with all the saints what is the breadth and length and height and depth, [19] and to know the love of *Christ* which surpasses knowledge, that you may be filled up to all the fullness of *God*."

To those words we might add his doxology written to the Corinthians:

II Corinthians 13:14 – "The grace of the Lord *Jesus Christ*, and the love of God (*the Father*), and the fellowship of the *Holy Spirit*, be with you all."

ENDNOTES

1. The philosophical and epistemological formulations of God in the Christian *theologia* section of this study are not original or unique to the author of this document. Additional study might be conducted in the writings of Scottish Reformed theologian, Thomas F. Torrance (cf. *The Christian Doctrine of God: One Being Three Persons*); German Catholic theologian, Karl Rahner (*The Trinity*); German Protestant theologian, Christoph Schwöbel (*Trinitarian Theology Today*); and American feminist Catholic theologian, Catherine Mowry LaCugna (*God for Us: the Trinity and the Christian Life*). They have noted how historic Christian thinking about God has tended to piggyback on early Greek philosophical constructs rather than proclaiming the distinctive Self-revelation of God in the person of the Son, Jesus Christ, revealing the unique relationality of the tri-personal Triune God.

2. During research and reading for the *theologia* section of this study I enjoyed and appreciated the writings of Dr. Martin M. Davis on his blog "God For Us," which can be found at http://martinmdavis.blogspot.com. He has an inimitable ability to explain theology in a down-to-earth manner.

3. Concepts expressed in the categories of *oikonomia* and *koinonia* were enhanced by reading articles by Kerry S. Robichaux, Ron Kangas, Ed Marks, Paul Onica, John Pester, and Witness Lee in *Affirmation & Critique: A Journal of Christian Thought*, a publication of Living Stream Ministry, http://www.affcrit.com.

Addenda

The illustrations that comprise the addenda of this document were originally used as visual projections on a screen that allowed the audience to visualize what could have otherwise been rather abstracted reasoning.

They are included in this book for the same purpose of allowing the reader to have visual diagrams of the thought processes contained in this treatise, and to see the flow of thought from category to category.

It is a valid truism that states, "A picture (or a visual) is worth a thousand words."

theologia

- human considerations and understanding of God.

oikonomia

- the administrative workings of God in human history in His Self-revelation via His Son, Jesus Christ.

koinonia

- personal relationship of participation with the Triune God and with one another in the Christian community.

Philosophical Ideal

FORM   **The One** (Tŏ″Ev)   Ultimate Reality

Eternal Forms   IDEA   The Really Real

First Principles   The Ideal   The Truly True

First Cause   Supernatural

Uncaused Cause   Universal Mind   Supreme Power

Perfect Ideal   Noumena   Omnipotent

         Thought behind all   Sovereign

Spirit/Soul   Almighty

of ALL

Archetype - Prototype   **BEING**   GOD

Essential Substance   *Ground of all Being*   Creator

Primary Virtue   *Non-contingent Being*   Singular Source

Categorial Core   *Metaphysical*   IntelligentDesigner

Prime Mover   *Abstract - undifferentiated*   Sacred

Unmoved Mover   *Intangible Originator*   Perfection

A priori methodology

Postulate   Hypothesize
Propose   Conceptualize
Project   Idealize
Speculate   Visualize

The superlative:
The best the human mind can reason.

Addendum C

Plato

428–328 B.C.

A priori

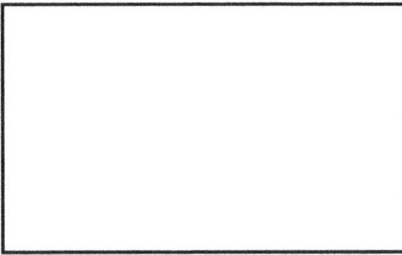

Aristotle

384–322 B.C.

A posteriori

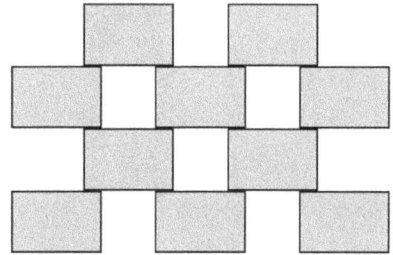

Plato	Aristotle
ideas	things
forms	manifestations
reality	appearances
being	becoming
archetype	ectype
mind	matter
conceptual	perceptual
spirit/soul	body
metaphysical	physical
noumena	phenomena
objective	subjective
supernatural	natural
God	world

Deductive Reasoning Process

universal ⟶ particular
general ⟶ specific
intangible ⟶ tangible
abstract ⟶ concrete

Inductive Reasoning Process

universal ⟵ particular
general ⟵ specific
intangible ⟵ tangible
abstract ⟵ concrete

Christianized
Philosophical TRINITY

FORM   Archetype - Prototype   Ultimate Reality

GOD

FATHER | **SON** | **HOLY SPIRIT**

BEING

Classical Theism
Natural Theology

I Cor. 1:20,21 - "The wisdom of this world does not know God."
I Cor. 2:14 - "The natural man cannot understand spiritual things"
I Cor. 3:18-20 - "The wisdom of this world is foolishness before God."

John 1:14 - "The Word became flesh..."
John 10:30 - "I and the Father are One."
Matt. 28:19 - "in the name of the Father, the Son, and the Holy Spirit.

Augustine

A.D. 354-430

A priori

Omni-god	Unity	Immutable
Omnipotent	Oneness	Unchangeable
Omniscient	Singularity	Inscrutable
Omnipresent	Simplicity	Impassibility
Father	**Son**	**Holy Spirit**
Independent	Aseity	Self-
Autonomous	Necessity	generating

Deductive reasoning

God is primarily viewed in His monotheistic oneness, *De Deo Uno*. The three-ness of the Trinity, *De Deo Trino*, must simultaneously be taken in account. So, the one God is basically presented as having three parts – a tripartite, trichotomous god.

In *De Trinitate*, Augustine repeatedly uses the analogy of the human mind as the deductive means of explaining the Trinity: memory, thoughts, and will

Is this a god after our own making?

Thomas Aquinas

A.D. 1225-1270

A posteriori

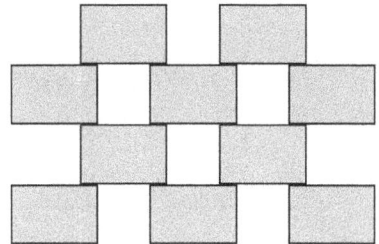

Inductive reasoning

Proofs of God's existence:
• Motion - movement requires a mover.
 God is the "unmoved Mover."
• Cause - everything has a cause.
 God is the "uncaused Cause."
[a] Existence - requires previous existence.
 God is the non-contingent Being.
• Gradation of value - greater creates lesser.
 God is the absolute moral perfection.
• Purpose - requires a purposer.
 God is the intelligent designer, the
 guiding hand that provides objective.

Classical Theism
Natural Theology

Addendum F

Athanasius

Council of Nicea

A.D. 325

Father and Son - one Being
homoousion to Patri

Cappadocian Fathers

Council of Constantinople

A.D. 381

one substance (*ousia*)
in three persons (*hypostaseis*)

GOD is NOT Trisected Into a Trichotomous, Three-part GOD

The Persons of the Trinity are NOT the "Front Men" for GOD

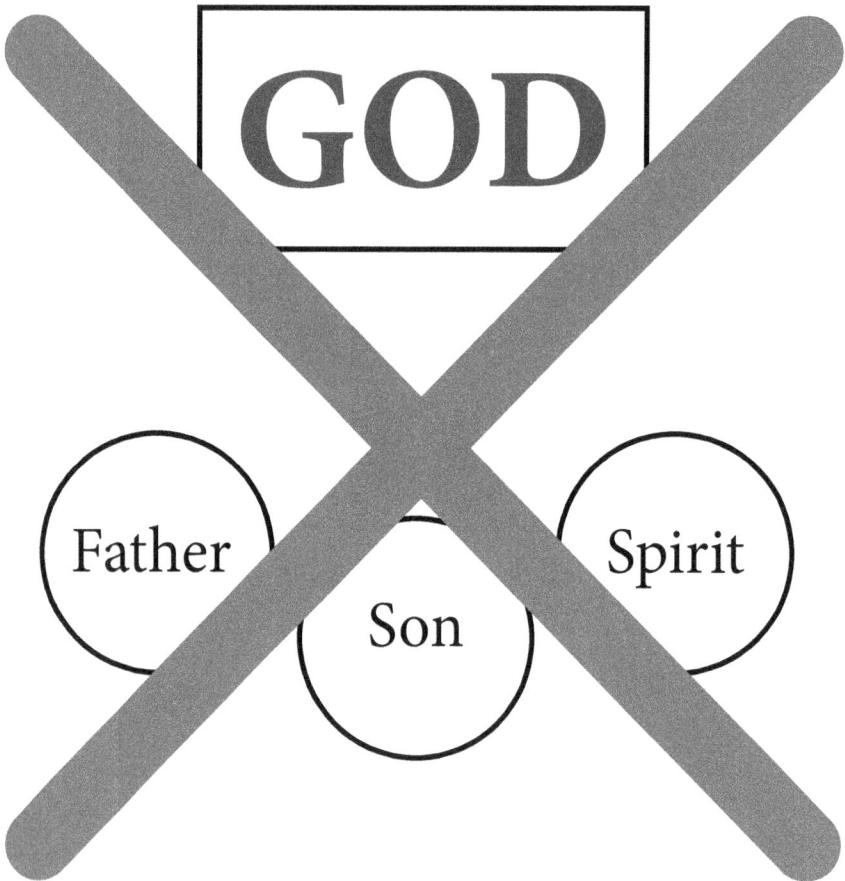

GOD

Father

Son

Spirit

Relational Understanding of the BEING of the Triune God

*The **Being** of God is revealed in the interrelations of the Father, Son, and Holy Spirit – historically revealed in space and time by the divine-human mediator, Jesus Christ.*

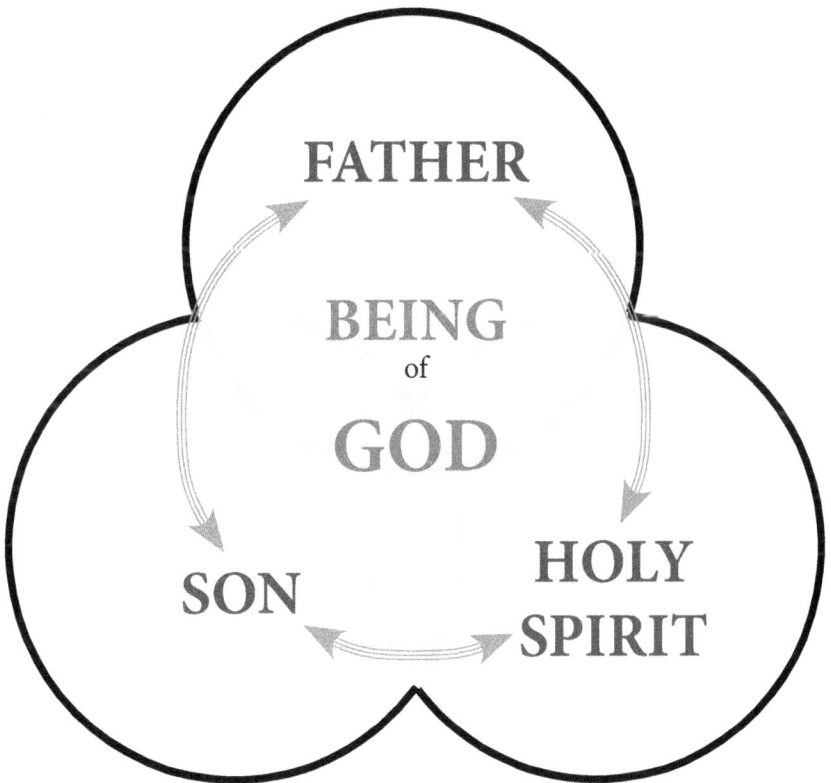

FATHER

BEING
of
GOD

SON

HOLY
SPIRIT

oikonomia

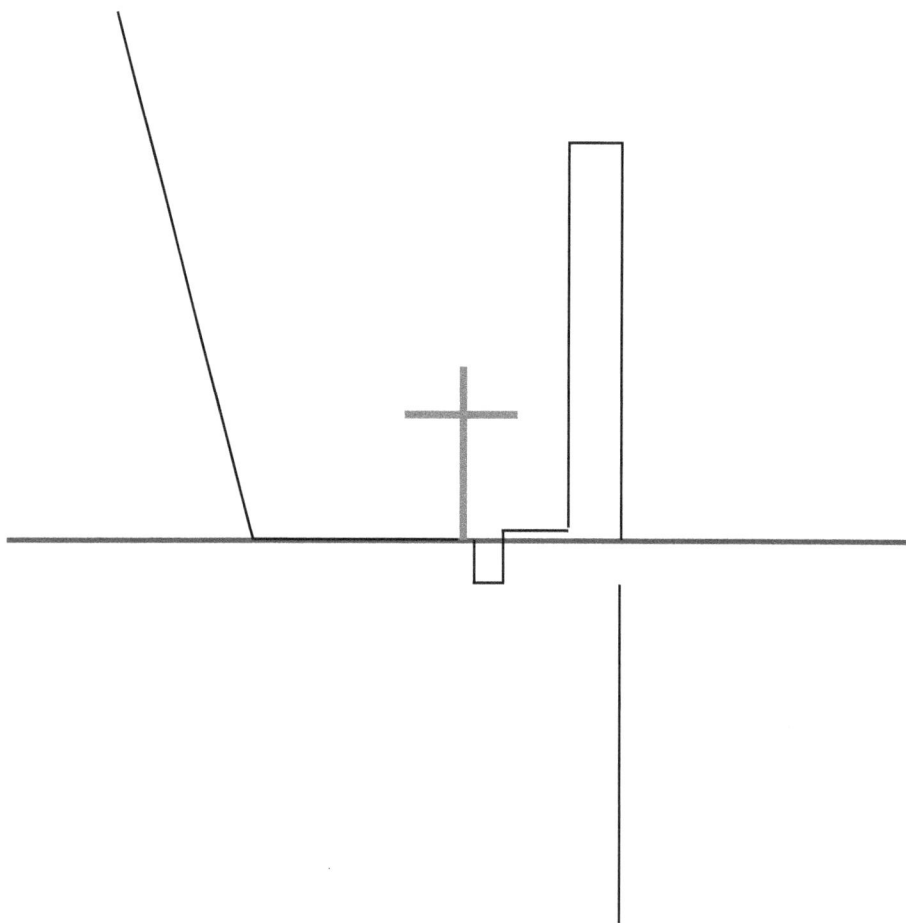

koinonia

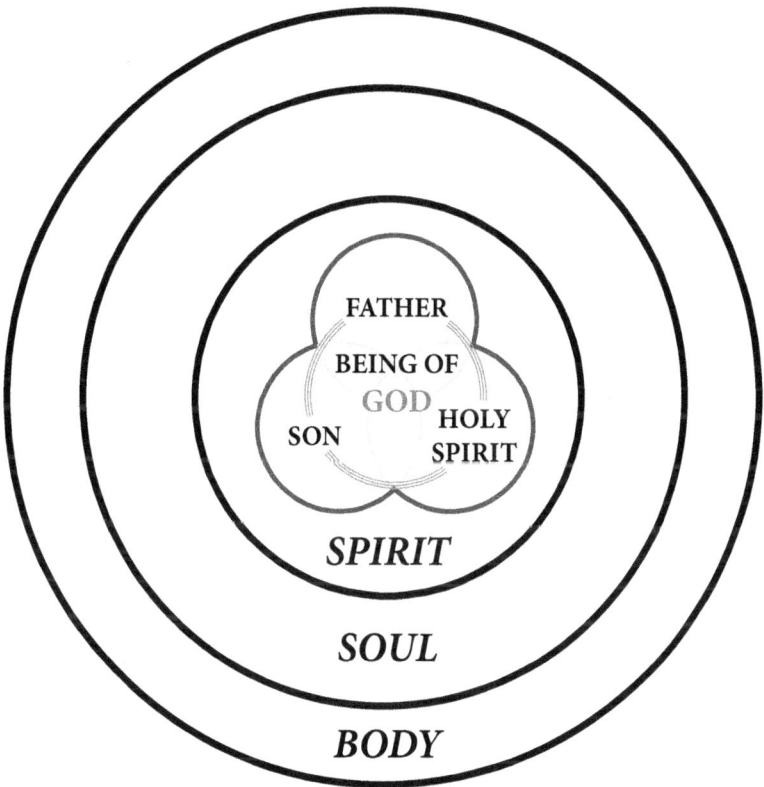

Trinity Indwelling
Human Beings

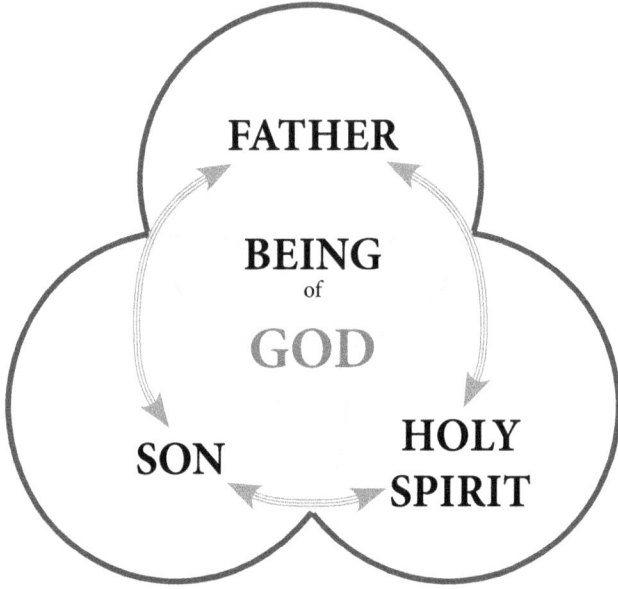

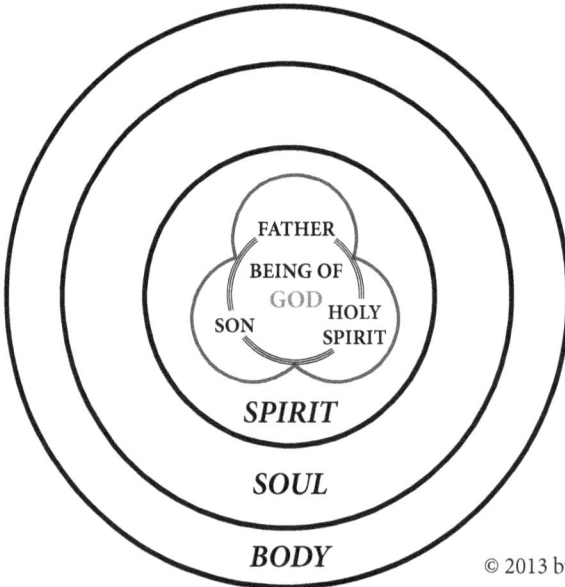

FATHER

BEING
of
GOD

SON

HOLY
SPIRIT

FATHER

BEING OF

GOD

SON

HOLY
SPIRIT

SPIRIT

SOUL

BODY

The Triune God
Made Available to Human Beings

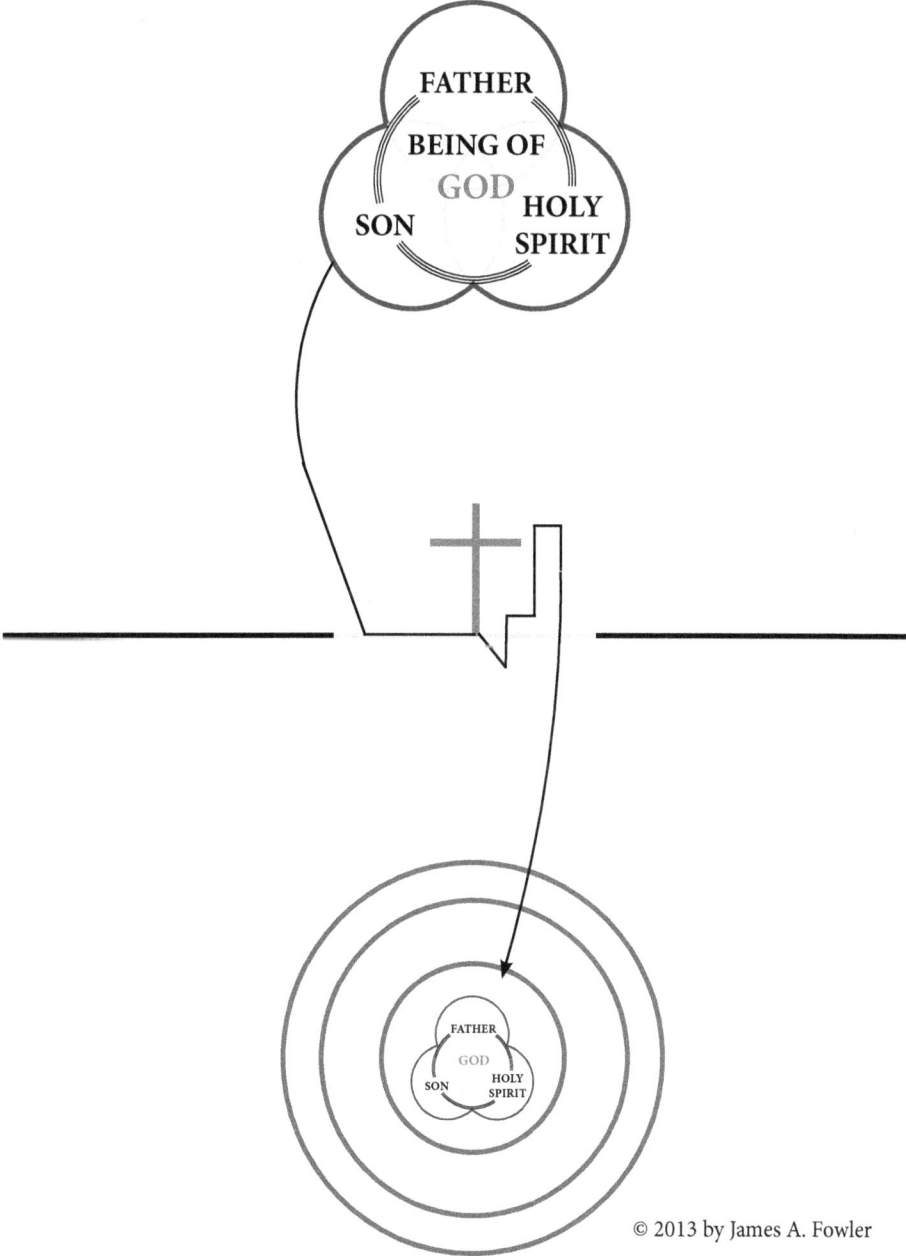

FATHER

BEING OF

GOD HOLY
SPIRIT

SON

FATHER
GOD
SON HOLY
SPIRIT

theologia	*oikonomia*	*koinonia*
God in Himself	God at work in history	God at work in us
Triune God in Christian thought	Triune God historically revealed in the Son	Triune God in Christian experience
theological speculation	historical manifestation	personal appreciation
speculation about God	revelation of God	participation in God
human consideration of God	redemptive work of God in Christ	personal fellowship with God
philosophical theology	redemptive theology	spiritual theology
Immanent Trinity - ontological Trinity - essential Trinity	Economic Trinity - operational Trinity - administrative Trinity	Conjunctive Trinity - perichoretic Trinity - union with Trinity
Relational and internal interaction of Triune God *a se*	Self-communication of Triune God *per adventum*	Relational Self-communication of Triune God *ad diversum*
apophatic theology "apart from speech"	*kataphatic* theology "according to speech"	*eisophatic* theology "to speak into"
Unknowability of God Mystery of God	Historic knowability of God via Revelation	Intimate personal knowing of God by personal revelation

Correlation of
the Three Categories

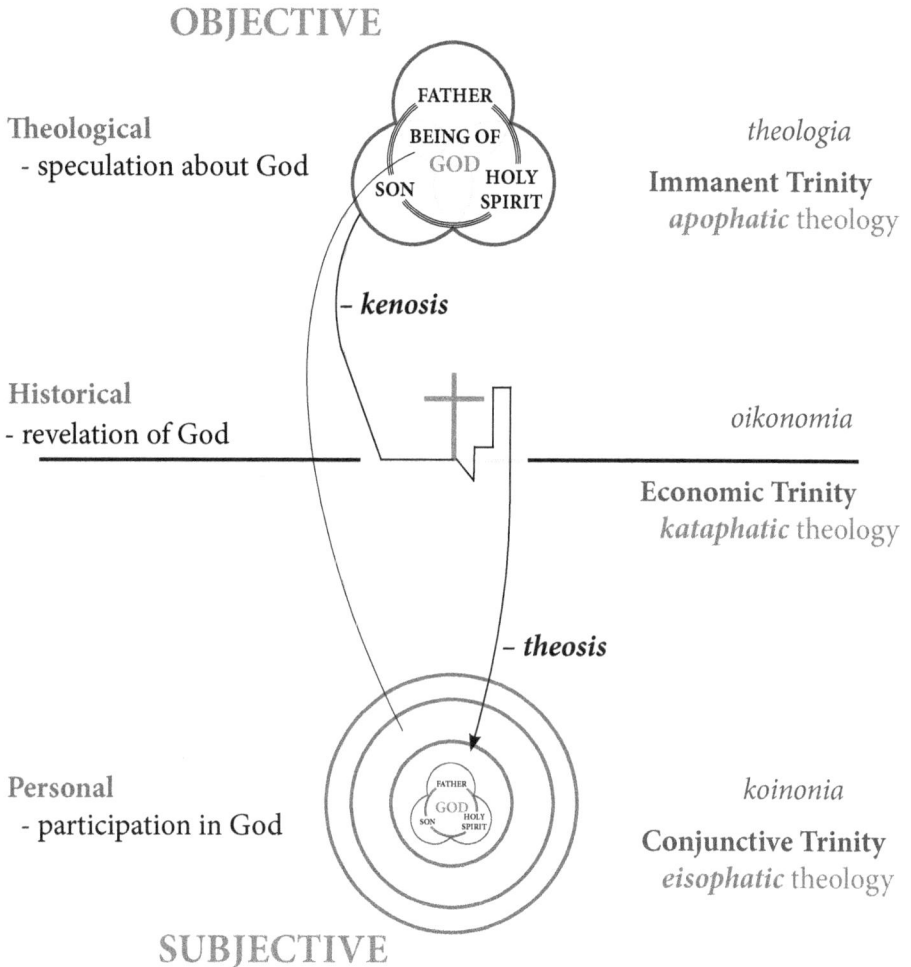

OBJECTIVE

Theological
- speculation about God

FATHER
BEING OF
GOD
SON HOLY SPIRIT

theologia

Immanent Trinity
apophatic theology

– kenosis

Historical
- revelation of God

oikonomia

Economic Trinity
kataphatic theology

– theosis

Personal
- participation in God

FATHER
GOD
SON HOLY SPIRIT

koinonia

Conjunctive Trinity
eisophatic theology

SUBJECTIVE

Christocentric Emphasis
of God's Revelation

The Triune God
in Christian Thought

theologia

provides the **data**
whereby we "know
about" God
philosophically.

The Triune God
Revealed in the Person
& Life of Jesus Christ

oikonomia

provides the **dynamic**
whereby we "know"
God personally in
participatory intimacy.

The Triune God
in Christian Experience

koinonia

The Triune God in Us
and Our Participation
in the Triune God

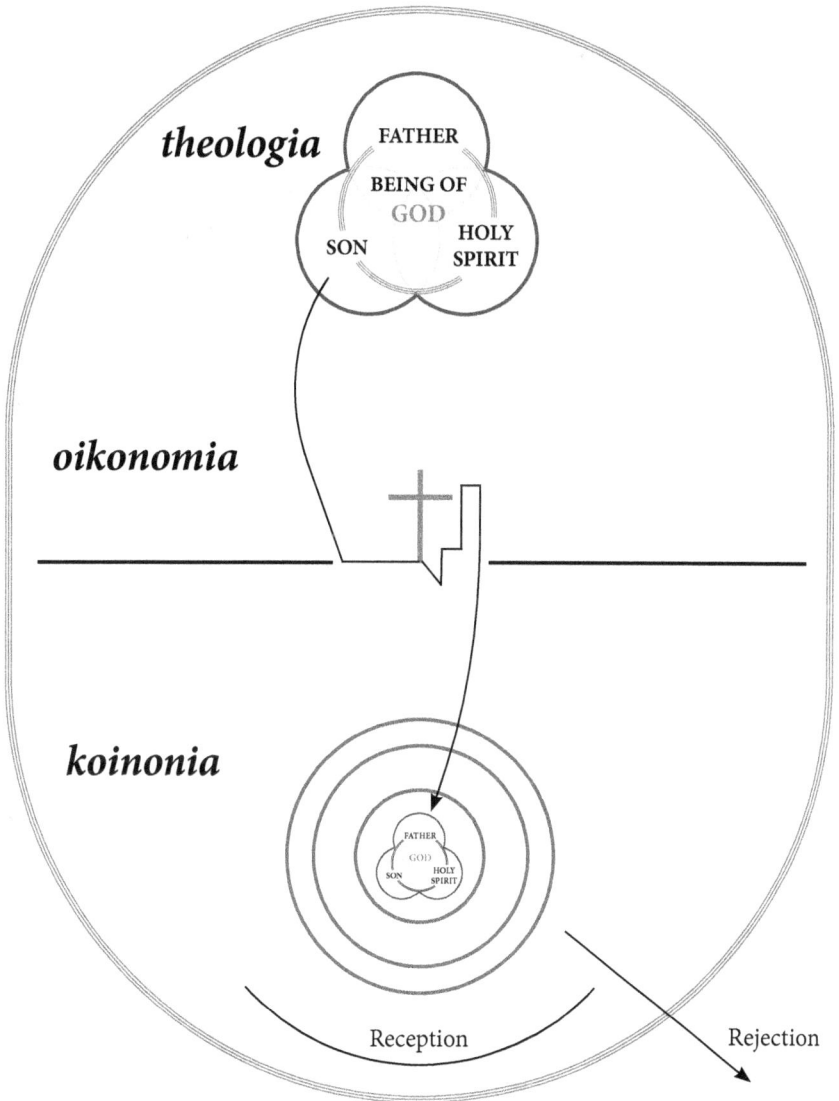

theologia

FATHER

BEING OF
GOD

SON

HOLY
SPIRIT

oikonomia

koinonia

FATHER

GOD

SON

HOLY
SPIRIT

Reception

Rejection

Humanity in the Trinity

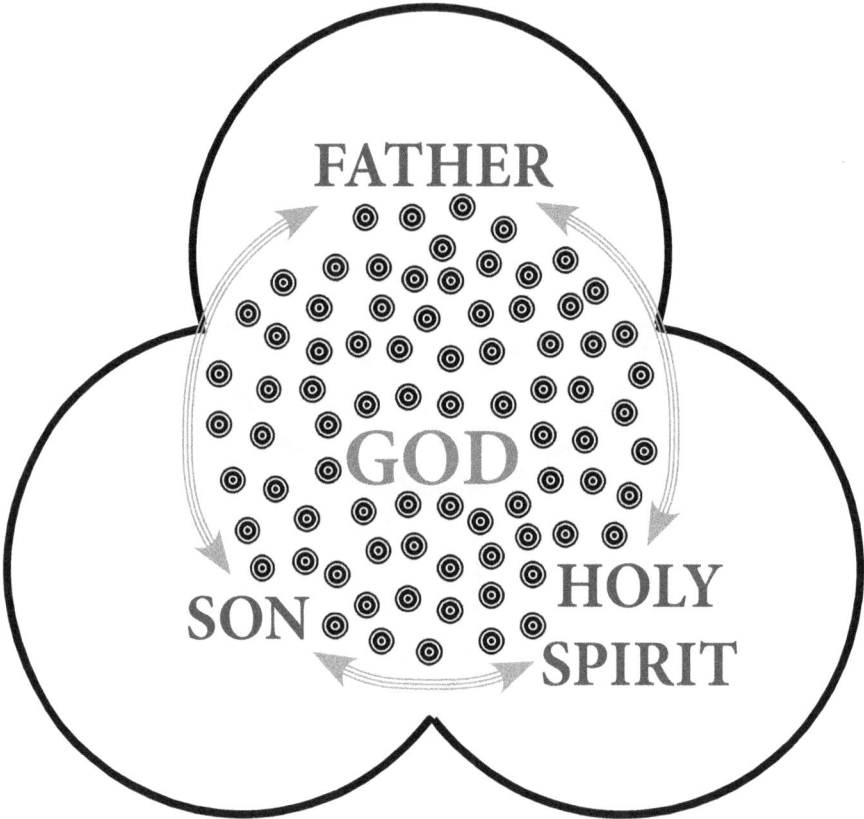

www.ingramcontent.com/pod-product-compliance
Lightning Source LLC
Chambersburg PA
CBHW060937040426
42445CB00011B/897